IMAGES
of America

SAN CARLOS

IMAGES
of America

SAN CARLOS

Nicholas A. Veronico and
Betty S. Veronico

ARCADIA
PUBLISHING

Published by Arcadia Publishing
Charleston, South Carolina

Library of Congress Catalog Card Number: 2007925815

For all general information contact Arcadia Publishing at:
Telephone 843-853-2070
Fax 843-853-0044
E-mail sales@arcadiapublishing.com
For customer service and orders:
Toll-Free 1-888-313-2665

Visit us on the Internet at www.arcadiapublishing.com

This book is dedicated to Joe and Claire Bradshaw.

Beautiful San Carlos Park
High Class Property For Sale

THE SAN CARLOS PARK SYNDICATE offers to HOMESEEKERS and INVESTORS, Resident and Villa Lots, Orchards, Vineyards and Acreage, in the MOST BEAUTIFUL TRACT OF LAND on the San Francisco Bay Shore—Rolling, Picturesque and Grand—Beautiful Creeks, Trees, Ferns and Flowers. Streets are to be GRADED, MACADAMIZED, SEWERED and LIGHTED.

SPRING VALLEY WATER

Climatic Conditions Perfect—Picturesque and Charming Scenery—Excellent Transportation. Via Bay Shore Cut-off of the Southern Pacific.

30 MINUTES' RIDE FROM SAN FRANCISCO

IDEAL LOCATION—Commands view of the Bay. The Home Place for the Business Man, the Merchant, the Professional Man, the Banker and the Capitalist.
EDUCATIONAL CENTER—The Leland Stanford, Jr., University, Reid's School for Boys, Order of the Sacred Heart from Paris, France, for Young Ladies, Hoitt's Academy for Boys, Manzanita Hall Preparatory for Stanford or Eastern Universities, Girls and Boys' High School are all located within easy reach of this Property.
BUSINESS AND MANUFACTURING SITES—On Deep Water, with Excellent Shipping Facilities by Rail and Water controlled by this Syndicate.

For Further Information, Pamphlets, etc., Call on or Address

SAN CARLOS PARK SYNDICATE
Offices: 393a and 395a Monadnock Building   San Francisco, California

The San Carlos Park Syndicate ran this advertisement on the inside front cover of the November 1907 issue of *Sunset Magazine*. The advertisement outlines the many wonderful aspects of purchasing land in San Carlos. A century later, a train ride from San Carlos to San Francisco is still only 30 minutes. (R. Gozinya collection.)

CONTENTS

ACKNOWLEDGMENTS

The history of San Carlos belongs to everyone. To that end, a number of great people opened their homes, businesses, and personal collections to share their photographs and memories that make up this visual history of San Carlos.

The authors are indebted to: Ray Abrams and family, A&A Racing; David and Rachel Anderson; Dominique, Sheridan, and Dante Anderson; Robert Anderson; Pat Ashton, Beckman Coulter, Inc.; Ken and Sandy Baisa; Fred and Penny Bausch, the Clocksmith; Gordie Bell; Cynthia Benson, Varian; Kristin Bergevin; Biber family; Ray and Caroline Bingham; Joe and Claire Bradshaw; Rich and Arlene Bradshaw; Vincent Bravo; Sam Brown, Kelly Moore Paints; Crista Buckner; Anthony Bullock, Joe Bullock, and Claudia Leonard, Faulstich Investments LLC; Roger and Darlene Cain; Bill Carpentier; Julie Clark; C .K. Crowley, American Legion; Tom and Veralynn Davids; Tim Davis; Louise Debarbrie and family; Frisco Del Rosario; Jim Dillaman; Sam Dorrance, Potomac Books; Simon Elliott, UCLA Library Department of Special Collections; Dave Elms; Desirae Fromayan; Jeri Fujimoto, San Carlos Youth Center; Mary Gardner and Mike Matosich; Michelle Gaskin; Scooter Giacosa and family; Carol Gianuario and family; Richard Gozinya; Linda Ferguson; John and Carrie Follett; Marion Jaroszewski, Delta Star; Wayne Kennedy and Lorelei Maison Rockwell; Paul Kierstein, CH Motorcars; Bob Kissick; Vera Lindeburg; Dr. William Lipski; Mary Luthy, Beckman Coulter, Inc.; Reg and Janet McGovern; Jim Magnuson and family; Renee Mastrocco, Rockefeller University; Rich Mazoni; Matthew Mintz; Jo Anne Montoya; David Morrill; Lee and Dulcie Morrison; Kim Morse; Tina Murphy, L3 Communications; Carol and Roy Nordman, Antiques Then and Now; Christopher O'Donnell; Jeff and Chris Nielsen, Nielsen Automotive; Jan Peters; John Poultney, Arcadia Publishing; Bruce Rollins; San Carlos Chamber of Commerce (Cheryl Pomerenk, Kathy Rollefstad, Wendy Schettino, Ann Weiss, and Dick Cox); San Mateo County Airports (Mark Larson, Meena Sharma, and Don Haug); Kim Sanini, San Carlos School District; Rick Spohn; Bob and Jimmae Seely; Gene Suarez, Redwood City Public Library; Richard Vanderford and family; Armand and Karen Veronico; Tony and Kathleen Veronico and family; Marian Vinal; Jonah Weinberg, San Mateo County Transit District; Joe, Marcelle, and Cliff White; Denny Williams; Bill and Sue Wood; Kellyjean Zaritek; and Mark Zielinski, Kelly Moore Paints.

In addition, three written works about the city and people of San Carlos deserve your attention, and each is available for sale or through the library: *It Could Only Happen in San Carlos* by Margaret Price; *Through the Years in San Carlos* by Effie C. Mahany; and *San Carlos Stories: An Oral History for the City of Good Living* by Linda Wickert Garvey. Each, in its own way, provides a snapshot of the people, places, and events that shaped our town.

San Carlos is truly "The City of Good Living."

—Betty S. Veronico
Nicholas A. Veronico
San Carlos, California, 2007

INTRODUCTION

San Carlos, California, located on the peninsula halfway between San Francisco and San Jose, was once the home of a small village of people called the Lamchins, part of the Ohlone Indians, a tribe of the Costanoans. As European exploration of the West Coast began in 1542, the Lamchins lived simply and peacefully. The first outsiders the Lamchins met were the crew of the *San Carlos*, who sailed into San Francisco Bay captained by Lt. Juan Manuel de Ayala in 1775. As the presidios, missions, and pueblos were being established by Spanish military and civilian settlers, the Lamchins' lives began to change. By 1810, the Lamchins were decimated by disease, forced labor, and the introduction of a foreign lifestyle and religion in what they called a "time of little choice."

The actual origin of the naming of the city of San Carlos is unknown. It is believed to be from one of three sources: the first ship to sail into the San Francisco Bay, after King Charles III of Spain, or the Portola Expedition that discovered the bay on the Feast of St. Charles on November 4, 1769.

Capt. Don Dario Arguello was *commandante* of the Presidio in San Francisco from 1787 to 1791, and in 1814, he served as the ninth governor of Alta California. For dedication to duty, in 1795, the Spanish government granted Arguello 35,420 acres known as the Rancho de las Pulgas; however, the family continued to live at the Presidio in San Francisco. The land extended from the San Francisciquito Creek near Palo Alto to San Mateo Creek, to the bay marshes, to what is now Cañada Road.

Arguello's son, Don Luis Arguello, was the first native-born governor to serve under the Mexican regime. After Don Luis's death in 1830, his widow, Dona Maria Soledad Ortega Arguello, moved to an adobe home at the Rancho de las Pulgas, at what is believed to be the corner of present-day Cedar and Magnolia Streets. Dona Maria lived at the adobe until 1851, when she sold it and 200 acres to Timothy Guy Phelps. Phelps moved into the adobe home and later purchased an additional 3,500 acres from Arguello to raise cattle and wheat. The Phelps family, along with the Brittans, Hulls, and others, became very prominent families in San Carlos.

After incorporation as a city in 1925, San Carlos truly evolved into "The City of Good Living." Schools were built, police and fire departments organized, and homes sold as new residents moved in. The town took to the sister city program, adopting Croydon, Australia, and more recently, in the aftermath of 2005's Hurricane Katrina, Pass Christian, Mississippi. This effort was spearheaded by the San Carlos Chamber of Commerce and the San Carlos Ministerial Association in conjunction with city leaders.

San Carlos has played a major role as the birthplace of many of today's leading electronics firms—Ampex, Dalmo Victor, Eimac, Lenkurt, Litton, and Varian all got their starts in town. Delta Star, Kelly Moore Paints, Black Mountain Water, and a host of other businesses, some large, some small, have thrived in the city's business community. It is amazing how many companies in town are run by second and third generations.

San Carlos has strong aviation roots and a long association with the military, and has been home to two racing tracks. Three movie houses were located in town, and San Carlos was also home to the Circle Star Theater, where the biggest names in show business came to entertain.

Today the town boasts a new library, an adult activity center, and a youth center. San Carlos is home to the world-class Hiller Aviation Institute and Museum, which hosts its Vertical Challenge Helicopter Airshow each June. Many community events, such as Art in the Park, Hometown Days, Hot Harvest Nights, and the Art and Wine Faire bring residents together.

This book provides a photographic journey through the history of "The City of Good Living."

This painting depicts a small band of men, both Native American and Spanish, lead by Don Gasper de Portola, on a hilltop looking down at San Carlos. Many historians now believe the hilltop Portola stood upon was Sweeny Ridge in San Bruno, not San Carlos. (Seely collection.)

One

EARLY DAYS
SAN CARLOS
BECOMES A CITY

There were many people who helped shape the foundation of San Carlos. The first American to purchase land and inhabit the San Carlos area was Timothy Guy Phelps. In 1851, Phelps began purchasing land from the Arguellos' Rancho de las Pulgas, totaling 3,500 acres in all, where he raised cattle. In 1854, Phelps became involved in the local vigilance committee in an effort to uphold the law in San Carlos. Elected as the first Republican from San Francisco and San Mateo Counties, Phelps served in the state assembly from 1855 to 1857, and from 1858 until 1861, he served in the state senate, then was elected U.S. Senator and served from 1861 to 1863. He was the first president of the Southern Pacific Railroad from 1865 to 1868.

John Brittan, a hardware dealer in San Francisco, purchased 3,000 acres of the Rancho de las Pulgas, extending from Cordilleras Creek to Pulgas Creek and west to Cañada Road. Upon his death, Brittan's three children each inherited a third of the estate. John's heir Nathaniel became the most notable of the Brittans with regard to the foundation of San Carlos. Nathaniel, his wife Isabel, and their three daughters, Carmelita and twins Belle and Natalie, lived in a beautiful home on Pine Street and often entertained at lavish parties. Nathaniel Brittan, owning the property on which the railroad was to pass, granted right-of-way through his land with the stipulation that a station agent and telegraph office be maintained at all times. In 1888, the city's train station was built.

Several attempts were made to form a city, the first in 1888 by the San Carlos Land Company, then in 1907 by the San Carlos Park Syndicate. Finally the Mercantile Trust Company hired Frederick Drake in 1917 to develop the town. Drake was the most successful by improving the water supply, providing water to individual lots, installing gas and electricity, and paving the streets. "The City of Good Living," coined by Drake, was finally beginning to prosper.

In 1925, Edward R. (Pop) Burton, Asa Hull, Fred Drake, and John Cowgill petitioned to have the city incorporated. In June 1925, the citizens of San Carlos voted to incorporate; in 1932, the fire department incorporated. The city continued to grow, the population increased, housing developed, and businesses prospered.

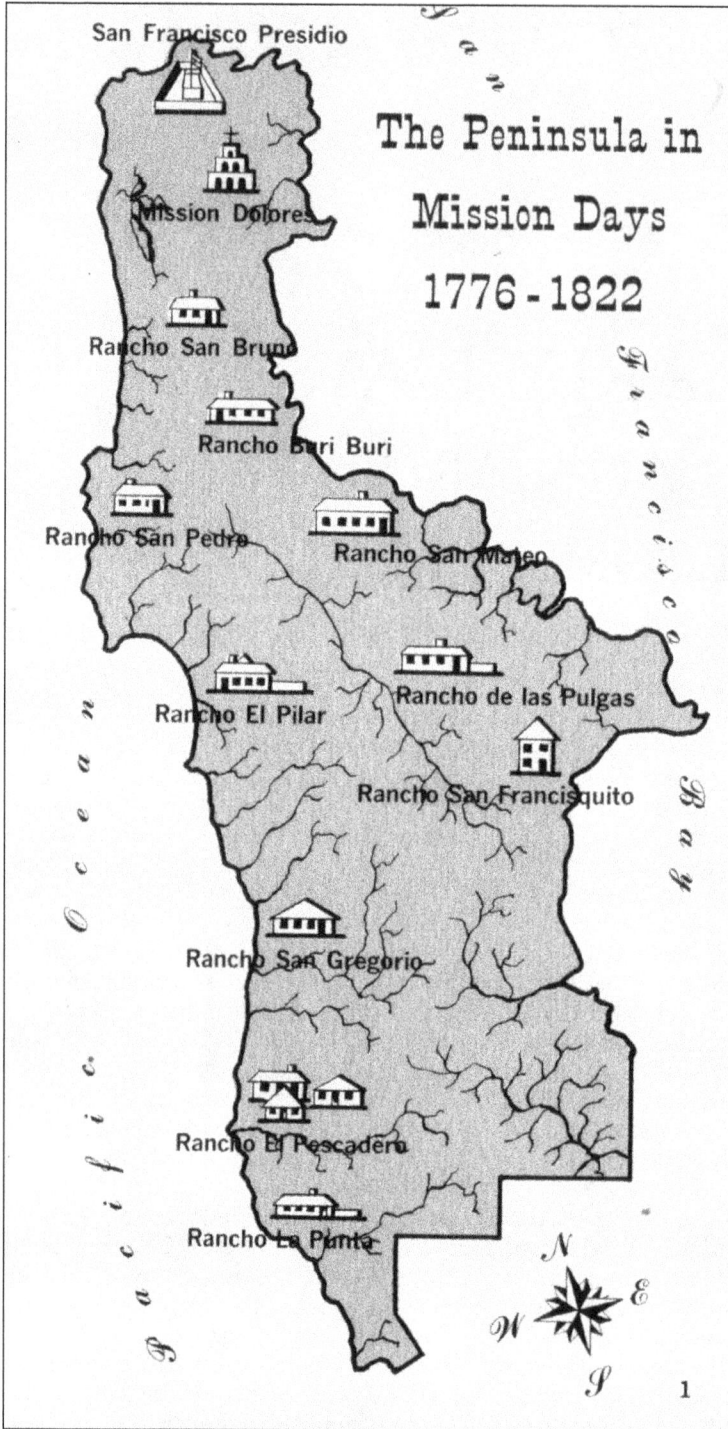

The Peninsula in Mission Days 1776-1822

San Francisco Presidio

Mission Dolores

Rancho San Bruno

Rancho Buri Buri

Rancho San Pedro

Rancho San Mateo

Rancho El Pilar

Rancho de las Pulgas

Rancho San Francisquito

Rancho San Gregorio

Rancho El Pescadero

Rancho La Punta

San Francisco Bay

Pacific Ocean

N E W S

1

This map depicts all the ranchos that were established on the San Francisco peninsula between 1778 and 1822. What is now the City of San Carlos was part of the Rancho de las Pulgas. (R. Gozinya collection.)

The San Carlos Park Syndicate was formed in 1907 in an attempt to develop a city. The map shows the corporation's vast holdings, which reached the San Francisco Bay at Steinberger's Slough. Note that the downtown area was already developed, and the syndicate's land began behind what is today Cedar Street. (Seely collection.)

The western portion of the San Carlos Park Syndicate land ran from downtown San Carlos through the hills to Spring Valley Lake, now known as Crystal Springs Reservoir. (Seely collection.)

The entrance to the San Carlos Park Syndicate's land was graced by this beautiful entranceway across from the train depot. (Seely collection.)

The San Carlos Park Syndicate office was opened to sell parcels of land. Note that the street and sidewalks near the office are finished and a fire hydrant has been installed to give a positive impression of the area to prospective home buyers. (San Carlos Chamber of Commerce.)

Potential home buyers arriving by rail at San Carlos were greeted by this idyllic scene of the depot against the eucalyptus tress. In 1864, the San Francisco–to–San Jose railroad was being constructed, and a right-of-way through San Carlos was granted by landowner Nathaniel Brittan with the stipulation that a station agent and telegraph office be maintained at all times. In 1888, Leland Stanford, a friend of Brittan, arranged to have his university's stonemasons build the depot. Almaden sandstone blocks, the same material used for many buildings at Stanford University, were used in the construction of the Richardson Romanesque Revival–style building—rare for a train station. The depot has served as a church, post office, and library, and is currently a café. The building was designated a city landmark in 1976, and in 1984, it was added to the National Register of Historic Places, No. 84001191. (Seely collection.)

While the Alameda de las Pulgas is currently a busy thoroughfare of San Carlos, it began as a simple tree-lined dirt pathway. (Seely collection.)

This is a photograph of the first home built on Cypress Street, now known as San Carlos Avenue. (Seely collection.)

Nathaniel Brittan joined the Bohemian Club in 1874. Eighteen years later, as president of the club, he had planned to donate a portion of his estate to the group for an out-of-town retreat. A cornerstone for the project was laid at Elizabeth and Orange Avenue. The project did not come to pass, and the Bohemian Club built its retreat at Northern California's Russian River. Brittan did, however, build a lodge at what is now 125 Dale Avenue. The two-and-a-half story building is octagonal in shape and has a 900-square-foot room where a number of Bohemian Club gatherings were held. The home, now a private residence, is listed on the National Register of Historic Places, No. 94001500. (Author's collection.)

As the San Carlos Park Syndicate sold lots, beautiful homes and manicured yards slowly began to appear. (Seely collection.)

Nicholas T. Smith, a Hudson River steamer captain, moved to California in 1852 with Leland Stanford to sell supplies to miners. Smith, accompanied by his wife, Mary Hooker Smith, came to San Carlos when the town was being developed. The couple built and lived in this beautifully landscaped home on the northwest corner of Laurel Street and San Carlos Avenue, known at the time as Cypress Avenue. (Seely collection.)

Capt. Nicholas T. Smith built this home, known as the Pagoda House, as a retreat from the constant pressures of people asking for funding for various projects. The home served as a private place where Smith and his cohorts could escape to play poker. Although it has been modified through the years, the home still stands at 300 Chestnut Street. (Seely collection.)

Pictured are the gates to Laurelwood, a beautiful estate owned by J. W. Bourdette of the California Brewers' Association. (Seely collection.)

A lone buggy travels down County Road bordering San Carlos Park, *c.* 1907. (Seely collection.)

Timothy Guy Phelps, originally engaged in the mercantile business in San Francisco, purchased 3,500 acres of land in San Carlos in 1851, became a California state senator, served in Congress, was the collector of customs in San Francisco, and was a regent of the University of California, Berkeley. Phelps, beloved by all that knew him, died on May 30, 1899, after being hit by two boys riding a tandem bicycle on Old County Road. (R. Gozinya collection.)

Pictured is the home of Timothy Guy Phelps and his wife, Josephine A. Phelps. The mansion stood north of Holly Street and east of Old County Road. A number of pine trees planted by Phelps on the property still stand in the area. (Seely collection.)

John Brittan, a hardware dealer from San Francisco, fell in love with the San Carlos area and purchased 3,000 acres of the Arguello estate. He built his home on what is now the corner of Elm Street and St. Francis Way. Upon Brittan's death, his three children, William, Nathaniel, and Mary Bertha, each inherited a third of the estate. Nathaniel was the most prominent San Carlos figure of the Brittan children. Pictured is Nathaniel's home, located at 40 Pine Street. The home had elaborate gardens, one of which housed a pit for a bear acquired on one of his Alaskan trips. (R. Gozinya collection.)

Brittan's mill, located on Chestnut Street on the Brittan family estate, was one of many windmills and water tanks used as the sole source of water for the city up until the 1920s. (Seely collection.)

William Hull, a brick maker, purchased 40 acres in San Carlos from Timothy Guy Phelps in 1858 for the good quality clay found in the area. The bricks made in San Carlos were used for many buildings throughout the Bay Area, including Fort Mason, the Palace Hotel, San Quentin Prison, and many others. William and Roseanna Hull, seated, had four children: from left to right, Asa, Guy, Mary, and Henry. Guy started a dairy in 1885 but decided railroad work was his calling and turned the dairy over to Asa, then only 15 years old. Mary wed Richard Shields, and Henry worked as a baggage master at the San Carlos train depot until his accidental death in 1904. Following his success as a dairy farmer, Asa went on to become the third mayor of San Carlos. (Seely collection.)

This home, located on the corner of Elm and Holly Streets, was originally built and owned by building contractor William Kreger in the early 1890s. In January 1923, the home, then owned by Charles Marvin, went up in flames and burned to the ground. The fire at this home was the catalyst for starting the volunteer fire department in San Carlos. (Seely collection.)

This map outlines the Oak Park area of San Carlos. The current-day streets include El Camino Real to the east, Alameda de las Pulgas to the west, Brittan Avenue to the north, and the property line followed what is now Belmont Avenue to the south. Oak Park is located between the Brittan Park and White Oaks neighborhoods. (Seely collection.)

A large lot in the Oak Park area of town would set a buyer back $300. Judging from the amount of cars near the Koff Realty Company billboard, lots sold quickly. (San Carlos Chamber of Commerce.)

21

On the edge of the San Carlos Syndicate property near the Alameda de las Pulgas was the Reid School for boys. In 1885, William Reid opened the semi-military-style boarding school for nine-year-old through high-school-age boys. While the school started small—about 25 students and one building—by 1891, the school covered more than 29 acres with many new buildings. The school, seen around 1910, was sold in 1918, and finally closed its doors in 1952. (Seely collection.)

A Dutch Colonial Revival–style home known as the Zeh House was named for Capt. George Zeh. In 1914, Zeh moved his family from San Francisco to San Carlos for his son Carl's health. While continuing to work in San Francisco, Zeh was one of the original suburban commuters. The home still stands at 700 Elm Street. (Author's collection.)

The San Mateo County game warden shakes hands with 17-year-old George P. Seely after he shot a lynx in an area of San Carlos known as Skunk Valley, near what is now the Brittan Avenue and Crestview Drive area. (Seely collection.)

The first school in San Carlos was organized in 1903. By 1916, classes were held in a home on the corner of San Carlos Avenue and Elm Street, and enrollment was approximately 20 students. Subsequently the city's first schoolhouse was built in 1918 at 650 Elm Street and accommodated eight grades. In 1930, this building became city hall. (San Carlos Chamber of Commerce.)

Looking east on Cypress Avenue, the train depot is flanked by two large urns. The large building to the left and behind the depot is the McCue Hotel, often called the Depot Hotel—although it never actually served as a hotel. Later the bottom floor served as a market while the upper floors became apartments. The hotel still stands today on the corner of McCue and Old County Road. The property to the right of the hotel was later used as one of the city's first airports. (San Carlos Chamber of Commerce.)

Two original buildings from the 1900s are pictured along the south side of the 1100 block of Cypress Avenue. These buildings still stand today, housing a popular restaurant (see page 76). (San Carlos Chamber of Commerce.)

Conklins, pictured here around 1915, was a stop for weary travelers on El Camino Real and was one of the town's first general stores. Residents could buy gas, bakery goods, and various other merchandise. They sold Red Crown gasoline, which began as a smokeless, odorless cooking fuel in 1890. Zeroline motor oil, the sign on the right pillar, and Red Crown were both products of Standard Oil of California. (San Carlos Chamber of Commerce.)

One of the first banking institutions in San Carlos was Bank of America. This early-1930s view shows the bank when it was located at the corner of Cypress Avenue and Laurel Street. Colocated with the bank was Best Buy Market. (San Carlos Chamber of Commerce.)

After the devastating fire at the Kreger home on February 23, 1923, the residents of San Carlos voted to form a fire district. The first truck was a taxicab chassis with a chemical truck body donated by the San Francisco Fire Department. The truck was housed at Wesley Mallory's auto garage on the corner of Holly Street and El Camino Real until the town raised money to build the first firehouse—less than a year after the formation of the department. Pictured here with a 1927 Seagrave fire engine and a hose and ladder truck are fire department members, from left to right, (first row) Eddie Lopez, Lyle G. Clark, Julies Edling, Edward J. Wheeler Sr., Harry Gee, Merritt Hosmer, and Gene Gorse; (second row) Henry Mahany, Henry F. Wrigley, Porter Heflin, Martin Cahill, Lee Dowd, Roy Collins, and Edward R. Burton Sr. The original fire station at 533 Laurel Street, seen in the background, was restored by the Lion's Club between 1979 and 1981 and gifted to the City of San Carlos. (San Carlos Chamber of Commerce.)

The Volunteer Fire Department's 1927 Seagrave fire truck is seen in action at the San Carlos Feed and Fuel Company in the early 1930s. Known as Engine No. 1, this truck, painstakingly restored by members of the San Carlos Fire Department, is driven in city parades more than 80 years after it was delivered. (San Carlos Chamber of Commerce.)

Built on the corner of Cypress Avenue (soon renamed San Carlos Avenue) and El Camino Real in 1929, this Spanish eclectic–style building was designed and constructed by Frederick Hugh Drake, also know as "the Father of San Carlos." Drake, hired by the Mercantile Trust Company, came to San Carlos in 1917 to build a city where the San Carlos Park Syndicate had failed. He succeeded in less than 10 years. This is the only remaining structure built by Fred Drake. (San Carlos Chamber of Commerce.)

The first post office in San Carlos was housed at the train depot in 1895. In 1926, the post office moved to what is now 734 El Camino Real, pictured above, with newly appointed postmistress Jesse Davis. A new building at 1150 San Carlos Avenue, below, was the home of the post office from 1936 though 1948, when it moved again to the 1300 block of San Carlos Avenue. The post office made its final move to its current location at 809 Laurel Street in 1958. The building at 1150 San Carlos Avenue still stands today, housing a restaurant and retail shops. (City of San Carlos.)

The 1915 Panama-Pacific International Exposition, held at the Marina waterfront fairgrounds in San Francisco, was the original home of the Ohio Building. It was built as an 80-by-113-foot replica, minus the dome, of the Ohio State Capitol. When the exposition closed in 1916, a group of investors purchased the building and planned to move it to San Carlos as the clubhouse for a proposed millionaire's playground. At low tide, the building was loaded into two barges and floated down the bay to its new home. (San Francisco Public Library.)

Arriving at San Carlos's Steinberger's Slough at high tide, tugboats positioned the barges into place and, at the following low tide, the Ohio Building settled into its new location. The awaiting foundation turned the building from a two-story to a three-story structure. The Ohio Building's surrounding property served as an airport in the late 1940s and early 1950s. A runway, hangars, and aircraft can be seen on the ramp behind the building. (Redwood City Public Library.)

This c. 1940 aerial photograph shows the pre–World War II development of the town of San Carlos. Many of the buildings, such as the train depot, McCue Hotel, the Drake Building, and

the original fire station on Laurel Avenue, still stand today. (Scooter Giacosa collection.)

You'll live better in...

San Carlos

The main photograph of this c. 1965 promotional brochure for San Carlos Estates looks down an undeveloped Brittan Avenue to the bay; the inset showcases the outstanding quality of life of San Carlos, with a family frolicking in one of the newly built homes' swimming pools. Pen-Pac Realty, then located at 336 El Camino Real, was the exclusive sales agent for the development. Homes were custom built to each owner's specifications by one of nine participating builders (Baywood Homes, Inc., Eastland-Kalend Construction Company, Vincent Errico, Henry Grambergu, Max Hansen and Sons, Inc., Marshall Development Company, James Saffores, Jack Scouten, and VeMAR, Inc.) cooperating on the project. (Author's collection.)

Two

The City of
Good Living

San Carlos has grown into a wonderful city since its incorporation in 1925. Many of the beautiful historic homes remain today, several of them still owned by descendants of the original families. Two grand examples are the homes at 371 and 408 Elm Street.

While some things go unchanged, most things do change. On San Carlos Avenue, two of the six buildings that comprised the Hacienda Garden Apartments were demolished and the remaining four were renovated, and the use has changed from residential to office space. To accommodate the continually growing city population, the Pacific Hacienda Condominiums were built on the location of the removed apartment buildings.

In the late 1940s, a disastrous fire destroyed the majestic Devonshire County Club at the top of Club Drive. The area has since been developed with single-family homes, condominiums, and parks, many of them with breathtaking views of the Bay Area.

Volunteerism has always been a strong value in the city, and numerous organizations contribute to the town's sense of community. Some of the organizations include the Rotary Club, San Carlos Women in Action, Lions Club, Kiwanis International, Quota International, Free and Accepted Masons, Civic Garden Club, and the San Carlos Chamber of Commerce. Without the volunteer members of these organizations, many of the city's wants and needs would not be met.

The ranks of the city professional service staffs, such as police, fire, and administrative, work hard to keep San Carlos a clean, safe place to live. The town's proximity to public transportation makes commuting a viable option for many of the city's residents.

"The City of Good Living" has played host to a number of events that have helped shape the foundation for many of the city's youth. The 1961 Babe Ruth World Series, won by the San Carlos team, developed three athletes who went on to become professional baseball players. The Miss San Carlos Pageant produced a number of young women who became, among other things, a professional airline and aerobatic pilot, an actress, corporate executives, and a governor of the state of Michigan.

The San Carlos community has always put its children and their education high on the priority list. The schools of the city are some of the best in the nation, many holding the honor of Distinguished School. Family and a sense of community are found throughout "The City of Good Living."

Nathaniel Brittan inherited a large tract of land that stretched from Brittan Avenue to Pulgas Creek to what is now downtown. When he subdivided the area, he named it Brittan Park. These pillars on the corner of San Carlos Avenue and Cordilleras Avenue mark the entrance to the property. (Author's collection.)

Located at 408 Elm Street, once known as Myrtle Avenue, is a beautiful Colonial Revival home constructed in 1912 by builder J. Wetzelberger. The original owner, Adolph Paulsen, a native of Denmark, was a well borer who drilled many of the wells in San Carlos and Belmont and was instrumental in the development of the water system for San Francisco's Golden Gate Park. Through the generations, the home has remained relatively unchanged and in the family of the original owner. (Author's collection.)

Pietro Valconesi built this San Carlos Villa at 371 Elm Street in 1928. It is believed to be modeled after the Italian villas of Valconesi's hometown near Genoa, Italy. The home's exquisite craftsmanship extends to the interiors where beautiful stenciling and murals grace most of the walls and ceilings. Upon completion of the home, Valconesi, on the steps of 371 Elm Street, purchased a new 1927 Buick touring car to add to his status in the community. (Kennedy/Rockwell collection.)

In 1934, Valconesi sold the home at 371 Elm Street to defray taxes. Antone (Tony) J. Zaepffel, owner of the Woodside Ice Company, purchased the home where he and his family lived until his death in 1950. From left to right are Tony, Elise, Alice, Louise, Anna, Alex, and Marie. (Kennedy/Rockwell collection.)

The Hacienda Garden Apartments originally consisted of six one- and two-story buildings set around a center courtyard and fountain. The apartments were built in 1931 in the Spanish eclectic style on the corner of San Carlos Avenue and Elm Street. In 2000, the city approved demolition of two of the buildings and renovations of the remaining four to professional office space. Much of the block surrounding the apartments was demolished as well to make room for the Pacific Hacienda Condominiums. (Author's collection.)

The Vanderford home on the corner of Cedar Avenue and St. Francis Way stands out from its neighbors for its unique architectural design. Built in the early 1940s, and seen here in March 1959, the two-story residence has an interesting octagonal-shaped living room among its many unique features. A number of oak trees that give the White Oaks area its name can be seen in the background at left. (Richard Vanderford family.)

36

Concerts in the park actually began in 1939 following construction of the Burton Park Amphitheater. One of the first performances of music in the park was organized and lead by concert musician Pasquale "Pat" Gianuario, also the town's barber. The Burton Park Amphitheater was the scene for many of the town's social events up through the 1970s. It was removed when the San Carlos Youth Center was built in the late 1990s. (Carol Gianuario family.)

This 1949 view of the corner of San Carlos Avenue and Laurel Street shows the crowd enjoying one of the many parades held in the city. The Carlos Theater is showing the first run of the Joan Crawford film *Flamingo Road* along with a Ma and Pa Kettle feature. Note the large number of servicemen in uniform. (American Legion.)

The Devonshire County Club was built in the 1920s at the top of Club Drive in the hills of San Carlos on land originally owned by Timothy Guy Phelps. The building was an English Tudor–style structure with great views of the San Francisco Bay. There were plans to build grand estates in the surrounding area, but those plans never materialized. The club was used for many of the town's social events, elegant dinners, and fund-raisers. From 1942 through 1944, the army built a dog-training center adjacent to the Devonshire Country Club property. The building was completely lost to fire in the late 1940s. (Reg McGovern.)

The San Carlos Police Department posed for its annual photograph on October 22, 1950, in front of city hall with its three squad cars, the chief's car, and its two motorcycles. From left to right are Sgt. Jim Edling, unidentified, Ed Whitney (kneeling), Officer Hosmer, unidentified (kneeling), Ed Bettencourt (kneeling), Tommy Thomas, Lt. George Seely (who became chief in 1953), Chief Ed Wheeler, city clerk Kathy Grant, Frank Lucero, Donald Lowe (kneeling), Jim Edling, and Ed Millard. In 1953, Lowe became a city building inspector. (Elwing Studios photograph via Seely collection.)

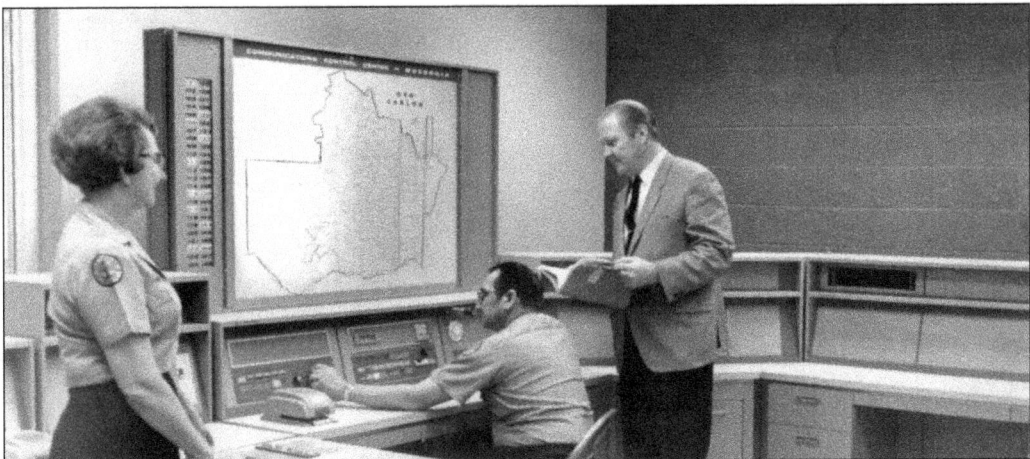

In 1960, San Carlos boasted a population of 21,370. To better serve its residents, the San Carlos Police Department upgraded its dispatch equipment from a typewriter and a radio to this then-state-of-the-art communications control center. Notice that one dispatcher (Joe Nagy, seated) has control of the entire city, and that the map shows that the west side of town has not been completely built out. Chief Joe Kimball, right, and Arlene Schlatter look on. (Seely collection.)

In preparation for the 1961 Babe Ruth League World Series in Glendive, Montana, the team was presented with new uniforms from the City of San Carlos. Pictured here are, from left to right, (first row) Dick Vinal, Mike Tyson, and Keith Woods; (second row) Bob Hooper, Ken Kambic, Rick Brown (who batted .588 in the league world series), Jim Magnuson, and Marty Redman; (third row) Coach Bob Flanagan, Bill Boles, Bill Laich, Steve Caria, Bob Pindroh, Jim McBride, Bill Alexander, Joe Judge Jr., and manager Bill Connolly. Seated in front is batboy Kerry Kambic. From this team, Steve Caria was drafted by the Orioles and Jim Magnuson was picked up by the Phillies. (*Tribune* photograph via Jim Magnuson collection.)

San Carlos's Bill Alexander beats the throw to third baseman Al Levithan on the Glendive diamond during the 1961 Babe Ruth League Championships. (Jim Magnuson collection.)

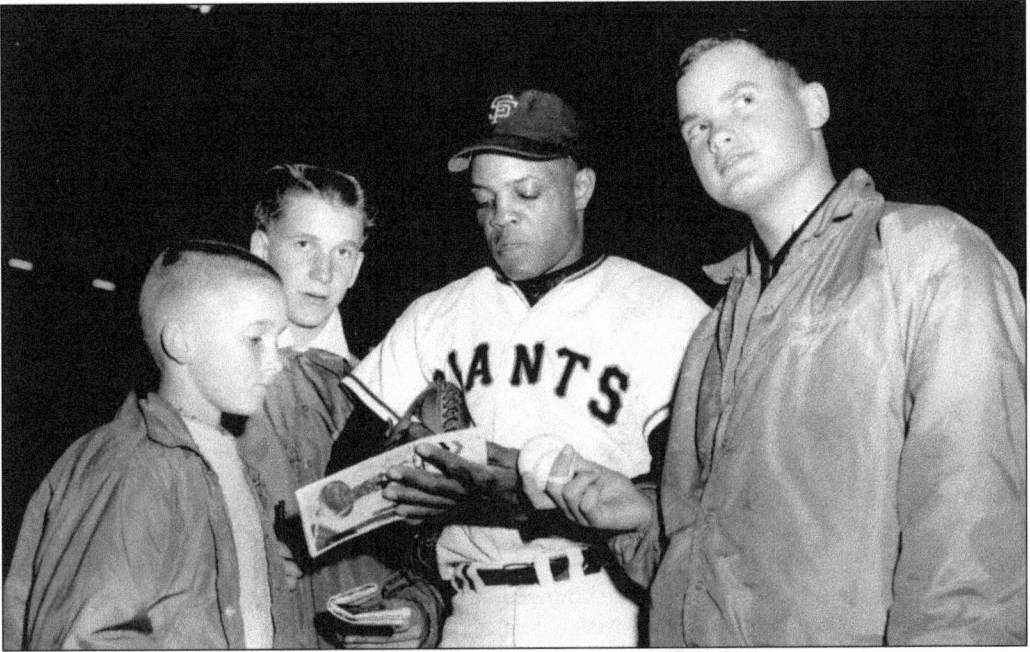

Being on the winning team has its privileges. Members of the 1961 Babe Ruth World Series team were invited to Candlestick to meet their idols. From left to right, Kerry Kambic, Mike Tyson, and Jim Magnuson spend a few minutes with San Francisco Giants great Willie Mays. (Newell Sharkey photograph via Jim Magnuson collection.)

Dick Stuart, a Redwood City native who played first base for the Pittsburgh Pirates, invited the team to Candlestick when he was in town on September 12, 1961. From left to right, Ken Kambic (kneeling), Bill Alexander, Bill Boles, Joe Judge Jr., Jim Magnuson, and Marty Redman surround the Pirates' first baseman. (Newell Sharkey photograph via Jim Magnuson collection.)

Miss San Carlos 1965, Linda Fenger, is surrounded by her court in the Burton Park Amphitheater. They are, from left to right, Leslie Kinsley, Jeanne Lawrence, Linda Fenger, Julie Clark, and Susan Taylor. The chamber of commerce sponsored the Miss San Carlos contest, which was often a stepping-stone to greater achievements in life for the contestants. (San Carlos Chamber of Commerce.)

Linda Fenger, Miss San Carlos 1965, receives the keys to a Triumph convertible sports car courtesy of Premier Imports, which was located at 1272 El Camino Real at Howard Avenue. Premier Imports gave each Miss San Carlos a car to drive for the summer months. After her time as Miss San Carlos, Fenger enjoyed acting in Hollywood, appearing in the movies *Beach Party, Beach Blanket Bingo, Muscle Beach*, and *Dr. Goldfoot and the Bikini Machine* among others. She went on to a career as an executive with Revlon, Estee Lauder, and later Cartier jewelers. (San Carlos Chamber of Commerce.)

In 1964, Julie Clark was chosen as San Carlos High School's homecoming queen, and in 1966, she was crowned Miss San Carlos. Clark attended UC Santa Barbara while advancing her pilot ratings and, in 1977, was hired by Hughes Air West airlines as the company's first female pilot. Through a number of mergers, what was Hughes Air West became Northwest Airlines, where Clark spent the majority of her career. She retired as a captain flying the Airbus A320 on November 25, 2003. Simultaneous to her airline captain day job, Clark has also flown her MOPAR-sponsored T-34 *Free Spirit* in a patriotic airshow routine for more than 25 years. (San Carlos Chamber of Commerce.)

Jennifer Mulhern Granholm was born in Vancouver, British Columbia, Canada, and moved with her family to the Bay Area in 1962. Granholm graduated from San Carlos High in 1977 and that same year was crowned Miss San Carlos. She later studied political science at UC Berkeley and received her law degree from Harvard in 1987. After serving with the U.S. Department of Justice, Granholm was elected attorney general of Michigan in 1998. She then ran for Michigan's highest office and was elected as its first female governor in 2002. (Reg McGovern.)

Visitors entering San Carlos from the south are greeted by the signs of the town's service organizations. This mid-1960s view shows Adeline Blessing and an unidentified gentleman after the addition of the Chicken's Ball sign (see page 81). (San Carlos Chamber of Commerce.)

On October 23, 1946, the Free and Accepted Masons of California, Lodge 690, was granted its charter, and Ferd Prince was installed as the lodge's first master. After sharing a temple with Redwood City Lodge 168 for several years, San Carlos Lodge 690 purchased the building at 1150 Arroyo Avenue in September 1948. Thor Madsen Plumbing and Heating occupied one of the ground floor units. Madsen ran his plumbing business from 1944 until he retired in 1970. He was later a San Carlos city councilman (1972 to 1976) and mayor (1974) and served on the parks and recreation commission for 12 years. In October 1984, the lodge paid off the mortgage and owned the building free and clear. After a devastating fire at the building that housed Lodge 168 in Redwood City and the closure of the San Mateo lodge, the three merged to become the Peninsula Lodge, No. 168, in San Carlos. (Peninsula Lodge 168.)

The 1941 San Carlos School second-grade class is pictured here with their teacher, Mrs. Chase. (Seely collection.)

Laureola School was built in 1951 on the location of the Timothy Guy Phelps carriage house—now Bayport and McCue Streets. With the decline in student enrollment, the school was closed in 1978, but the playground remains as what is now Laureola Park. The park is home to a ball diamond, basketball courts, benches, picnic tables, barbeque pits, playground equipment, a recreation center, restrooms, and a soccer field. (San Carlos School District.)

Located at 2757 Melendy Drive on more than 11 acres in the beautiful hills of San Carlos is Heather Elementary School. In 1963, twenty classrooms, a library, and administrative offices were ready for the K–6 students to begin their education. Today Heather School is a neighborhood public charter school serving students from kindergarten through fourth grade. (San Carlos School District.)

Arundel Elementary School, home of the Arundel Knights, held its first class on April 18, 1949. The original school consisted of the two upper-level buildings with 15 rooms. A multiuse room was added in 1956, and in 1961, the lower level was added. Construction continued through 2000 with the addition of administrative/staff rooms and a library media center. Arundel became a charter school in 2000. (San Carlos School District.)

Located at 2000 Belle Avenue, Brittan Acres School opened in 1952. Once a K–6 elementary school, it transitioned into a conversion charter school in the 1999–2000 school year, reducing classes to kindergarten through fourth grade. The school's main focus is to "build powerful readers and exceptional communicators." (San Carlos School District.)

Located on the corner of White Oaks Way and Cedar Street is the White Oaks Elementary School. Originally built in 1945 with just four classrooms, five additional classrooms, a library, and administration offices were added in 1947. In 1953, the school was enlarged again to include eight more classrooms. (San Carlos School District)

Opening its doors in 1953, Tierra Linda Middle School, located at 750 Dartmouth Avenue, schooled children in seventh and eighth grades. The school reopened in 2000, holding classes for fifth through eighth graders, approximately 485 students a year. (San Carlos School District.)

Central Middle School at 828 Chestnut Street was originally opened on September 20, 1930. Additions were added to the school in 1939, 1941, 1942, and again in 1960. Today the school serves approximately 520 students a year in grades five through eight. The auditorium of Central School is used for many of the city's activities, including the Chicken's Ball. (San Carlos School District.)

San Carlos High School, located on Melendy Drive, opened in 1960. Students were reluctant to attend the new campus, but sports activities helped ease the transition. By the late 1960s, as the Vietnam War escalated, San Carlos High became a turbulent campus. Because of a lack of students, the school closed in 1982, and the structure was demolished in 1988 to make room for new homes. (Above, Rich Bradshaw collection; below, Bruce Rollin.)

On Sunday, September 27, 1970, a 50-acre brush fire began in the Devonshire Canyon area. The fire started behind homes on Chesham Avenue and was out of control in five hours. Fire crews from Stanford to Marin came to lend mutual aid. The fire was threatening homes on the ridge of Melendy Drive, and a B-17 air tanker was called in to drop fire-retardant chemicals on the blaze. The bomber's second pass, at 5:30 p.m., knocked down the fire, which was under control by 9:00 that evening. This photograph was taken from the grounds of San Carlos High School. (Reg McGovern.)

With the opponent halfway around the world, Frisco Del Rosario, on the phone, relays the moves of Neville Arroues in a chess match with 14-year-old Jamie Galatas, a resident of San Carlos' sister city Croydon, Australia. More than 20,000 people watched the game in Croydon, where they erected a life-sized chessboard and, for dramatic effect, removed dead pieces on stretchers. Arroues won the game. The match, held in 1988, was the first event of the cities' cultural exchange program. (Dulcie Morrison collection.)

50

San Carlos Avenue is seen in the mid-1950s from two different angles. Above, on the left side, the Drake Building and the 1139 Club are visible, while a gas station occupies the northwest corner. The Carlos Theater, seen in the distance, was closed on September 14, 1976, and its demolition made way for construction of the savings and loan on Laurel Street, San Carlos Avenue, and Walnut Avenue. In the lower photograph, looking east down San Carlos Avenue from Laurel Street, is Lefty's news stand (where Starbucks is today), Owl Rexall Drugs (today's Sneakers Pub and Grill), and the 1139 Club (now Vic's Restaurant). (Above, San Carlos Chamber of Commerce; below, Mike Roberts/Paulson News Company.)

The C. C. Morse Seed Company acquired a large tract of land from the Brittan estate and maintained its San Carlos headquarters at 211 Bay Tree Road. The property was approximately 60 acres, which stretched from El Camino Real west to Chestnut Street between Arroyo and Brittan Avenues. Morse Boulevard is named for the flower-growing operation. Charley Wong, who later ran his own flower-growing business in the Devonshire Canyon area, was the property's first foreman. When the property's well went bad in 1929, Morse Seed Company (now Ferry Morse Seed Company) moved to Mountain View, California, and the property was subdivided as the San Carlos Gardens. (Author's collection.)

Three

BUSINESS AND INDUSTRY
THE BIRTHPLACE OF
SILICON VALLEY

Situated between San Francisco and Stanford University, San Carlos has always drawn some of the brightest engineering minds. These entrepreneurs set up shop in San Carlos in the 1930s and developed an electronics industry that was unmatched until the dot-com boom of the late 1990s. Companies such as Ampex, Dalmo Victor, Eimac, Lenkurt, Litton, and Varian dominated the electronics industry, and those that were not absorbed in the 1980s and 1990s have diversified into a wide range of products.

San Carlos is a town of tradition, where second and third generations are running the family business. These include Granara's Flowers, Lindeburg Jewelers, Neilsen Automotive, and Olsen Nolte Saddle Shop, to name only a few. As the generations have passed and new family leaders emerge, the businesses have grown to new heights.

Gone, but not forgotten, are businesses such as Woolworth's, located on the corner of Laurel and Cherry Streets; White Front, the 130,000-square-foot retailer that was situated on the east side of Industrial Road between Brittan and Howard Avenues; Peggy Lee's Creamery; and University Creameries, as well as two miniature golf courses—one by the Laurel Theater and the other at 204 El Camino Real. Super A Market and Laurel Super occupied the storefront on the corner of Eaton and Laurel Street, and Bell Market, at Laurel and Olive Streets, is now but a memory. Gone too are the funky fast-food joints, such as Pup 'n Hound at the corner of Holly Street and El Camino Real, and Foster's Freeze in the 800 block of El Camino.

In place of those nostalgic businesses comes new growth. Breuner's has been torn down to make way for PetSmart, Home Goods, Bassett Furniture, and a T. J. Maxx store. And the downtown area continues to evolve as well. Salvatore's Restaurant, formerly located at 1000 El Camino Real, has been removed, and a mixed-use building will take its place that will feature retail on the street level with residential above and off-street parking.

New technologies continue to be developed in San Carlos. Nektar Therapeutics is working on new drug delivery technologies for the pharmaceutical industry, and Tesla Motors is building a high-performance, 100-percent electric roadster capable of 0 to 60 miles per hour in about four seconds—at a cost less than 2¢ per mile. San Carlos business *is* innovation.

George Faulstich worked delivering milk until the Great Depression, when he changed to delivering water. He toiled for a few years at the Mountain Springs Water Company as its San Francisco peninsula driver. In those days, only the very wealthy or health-conscious drank bottled water. Faulstich located a spring by the side of the road on the Carolans Estate in Hillsborough. A deal was struck with the property owners, and shortly thereafter, in 1932, Faulstich started his own company, named after Black Mountain Road, where his spring was located. (Faulstich Investments LLC.)

By 1936, Faulstich and his wife had designed and built a home on Carmelita Drive, and George had located a natural-flowing spring at 800 Alameda de Las Pulgas in San Carlos. He immediately began acquiring property around the spring and moved Black Mountain Water to the site in 1939. Bottling facilities and the company's offices were located on the property. (Faulstich Investments LLC.)

Here's a good-looking promotional shot of Bud Hunt delivering a five-gallon bottle of water in the San Carlos Hills. Nearly 70 years after locating a spring on Black Mountain Road, the Black Mountain Spring Water Company was acquired by Great Spring Waters of America (part of the Perrier Group) in 2001. (Faulstich Investments LLC.)

Having a tamper-evident cap on a jug of milk or a bottle of water provides a sense of security in today's world. That cap was invented by George Faulstich to improve the bottling process at Black Mountain Water. After patenting the cap on February 11, 1964, Faulstich formed the Cap Snap Seal Company. The company was acquired by Portola Packaging in 1986. Here an in-line cap sealer seats caps onto one-gallon bottles on a conveyor. (Faulstich Investments LLC.)

Working on a grant from the Rockefeller Foundation to provide research to the Rockefeller Institute for Medical Research, Dr. Edward G. Pickels and his collaborators, J. Biscoe and Dr. Ralph W. G. Wyckoff, designed and built an air-driven ultra centrifuge for studying viruses and crystalline proteins. Dr. Pickels's work was done in one of the outbuildings at 1660 Laurel Street, where J&M Hobby House is now located. (Rockefeller University Archives.)

Seen here is the control panel and absorption camera of the ultra-centrifuge developed by Pickels et al. in San Carlos. This pioneering work has enabled researchers to find cures for a variety of diseases and develop tests for many others. Pickels later formed Spinco (Specialized Instruments Corporation), located in Palo Alto, to further his work on centrifuges. Spinco was sold to Beckman Coulter in 1954. (Reproduced from *The Journal of Experimental Medicine*, 1936, 64: 39–45; The Rockefeller University Press.)

Ideal Hair Cutting was located at 1213 San Carlos Avenue. Barber Pat Gianuario and two others worked in the shop, and one could get a haircut for only 25¢ in the early days. Although San Carlos had a city hall, many old-timers reported that most city business was unofficially conducted on these chairs. (Gianuario family.)

Barber Pasquale "Pat" Gianuario was a concert musician, a devoted lute player, and was extremely active in the San Carlos Community Theater before there was a Chicken's Ball. In 1939, Gianuario began giving concerts in the amphitheater at what is now Burton Park (named after Edward R. "Pop" Burton in June 1960). (Gianuario family.)

Located next to the Carlos Theater, the University Creamery was a popular stop after the movies. The creamery, owned by Chris Christiansen, had locations in Palo Alto and Redwood City as well. (Author's collection.)

Only the brand of gasoline has changed at the Nielsen family's service station. Built by George Nielsen Sr. in 1946, the station is now operated by the third generation of the family. As they did in the 1940s, the station still offers full service to motorists. This art deco–style station (General Arrangement Service Station design No. 2708) was based on architect Rudolph Schindler's 1933 Union Oil Company prototype design. Schindler was heavily influenced in his designs by having worked with Frank Lloyd Wright for more than five years. (Jeff and Chris Nielsen collection.)

In the late 1940s, Bay Center Motors was located in the 800 block of El Camino Real, next to George Nielsen's Union 76 station. Behind the car lot's offices is the Masonic Temple, and to the right can be seen the businesses along Laurel Street. Note that the hills west of town are undeveloped. (Jeff and Chris Nielsen collection.)

On August 16, 1950, a fire broke out at Chemical Associates on Old County Road north of Brittan Avenue. San Carlos, Belmont, Redwood City, and San Mateo firefighters worked from 8:30 p.m. to 3:30 a.m. to put out the fire, which destroyed the company's 12,000-square-foot plant. *Redwood City Tribune* staff photographer Reg McGovern snapped this photograph at the instant of an explosion. It would become 1950's most-honored news picture. (Reg McGovern.)

In 1932, Charles Litton started a small business at his Eaton Avenue home building microwave tubes. The company expanded during the war years and occupied two Quonset hut–style buildings on Brittan Avenue near Industrial Road. In 1952, Charles Litton sold the tube side of his company and retained the machinery manufacturing division (Litton Engineering Laboratories). The new owners called this acquisition Litton Industries, and the San Carlos facility was renamed the Electron Devices Division of Litton Industries. Of note, Litton Industries acquired San Carlos's Dalmo Victor in 1991. (L-3 Communications, Electron Devices.)

Litton Engineering Laboratories developed a lathe for making radio tubes of consistent high quality, as seen here inside the San Carlos facility. Not only did the company make its own tubes, it developed a line of glass-forming machines for industry. In 1953, Charles Litton moved the machinery division to Grass Valley, California. (L-3 Communications, Electron Devices.)

In front of the San Carlos facility in 1948, the original Varian team is, from left to right, Russell Varian, Sigurd Varian, Marvin Chodorow, Dorothy Varian, Richard Leonard, Esther Salisbury, Edward Ginzton, Fred Salisbury, Don Snow, and H. Myrl Stearns. The Varian brothers continued to build klystrons for the communications industry and the military while branching out to build other scientific instruments. (Varian Inc.)

Russell and Sigurd Varian pose with a large klystron tube in this famous Ansel Adams photograph, which appeared in *Fortune* magazine. (Ansel Adams via Varian Inc.)

In addition to Litton and Varian, Dalmo Victor was one of the early high-tech companies based in San Carlos. The key to the Allies' effort to defeat the German submarine menace of World War II was airborne radar. San Carlos's Dalmo Victor was instrumental in building the APS-6 airborne X-band search radar. This postwar advertisement shows a number of the components pioneered by the company. (Author's collection.)

A Dalmo Victor–built APS-6 airborne search radar is seen on a Grumman TBM-3E Avenger, BuNo. 53593, on display at the National Museum of Naval Aviation in Pensacola, Florida. The white pod under the starboard wing housed the radar antenna. (Author's collection.)

62

Alexander M. Poniatoff, right, founder of Ampex, used his initials and the letters "ex" for excellence to form the company's name. Ampex started by building small generators and electric motors and, after World War II, developed magnetic tape and recording equipment for both audio and video applications. Poniatoff is seen with a VR-1000 video recorder. Ampex's technical contributions have been recognized with an Oscar and 12 Emmy awards. (Redwood City Public Library.)

A sound engineer in Ampex's 1155 Howard Avenue facility prepares a recording. It is interesting to note that in 1944, Dalmo Victor occupied the first three floors of the old J. W. Brooks furniture factory on the corner of Belmont Avenue and El Camino Real, and Ampex was located on the top floor. (Reg McGovern.)

Precision Instruments was a San Carlos–based company that built tape recorders for scientific and military applications. NASA used recorders built by Precision Instruments extensively in the early 1960s, and the U.S. Navy employed them in antisubmarine warfare as well. (Author's collection.)

Eitel-McCullough, known as Eimac, began in 1934 in San Bruno building tubes for amateur radio enthusiasts. During World War II, they built radar and other electronic tubes for the military. By 1959, the company moved to a new facility in San Carlos on Industrial Road north of Holly Street. In 1965, Eitel-McCullough merged with Varian Associates and continued to build high-power vacuum electron devices. In 1995, the Eimac Division was acquired by Communications and Power Industries (CPI), Inc. The Eimac site is slated to become a new Palo Alto Medical Foundation campus. (Author's collection.)

In 1944, Lennart G. Erickson and Kurt E. Appert gave their names to Lenkurt Electric, a manufacturer of microwave and carrier equipment for the communications industry. A decade later, as the company grew, they engaged architects Frank Lloyd Wright and Aaron G. Green of San Francisco to develop preliminary sketches for a futuristic 200,000-square-foot factory that would employ 2,000. Employee parking was to be underground. The project was stopped in 1957, when Western Electric began talks to acquire the company. Lenkurt was located between Industrial and Old County Roads and Brittan and Howard Avenues. (Author's collection.)

TDY San Carlos

San Carlos, California?

Sure. On Lenkurt's San Carlos campus – where, for the past 14 years, we've been offering a CUS-TOMER TRAINING SCHOOL.

Nearly 4,000 students have completed as much as three weeks' intense instruction, and they're better communications men because of it. Classes are small to encourage greater individual comprehension of even the most complex subject.

Why do we keep on doing this? *Responsibility*: we feel the name Lenkurt must stand not only for a respected supplier of communications systems, but for a source of continuously available customer services, as well.

And it's this same sense of responsibility that guides our ENGINEER, FURNISH & INSTALL program, where we stand ready to plan, engineer, build, test, and service any communications system, anywhere.

Or our EQUIPMENT DRAWING & PUBLICA-TIONS INFORMATION SERVICE – offering com-

plete and current instruction manuals, specifications, bulletins, and technical drawings for all Lenkurt equipment. It's an almost endless source of engineering and operating information, created especially to fill your specific needs.

Even if you can't be assigned TDY at San Carlos, you can still receive our informative monthly *Demodulator*, presenting concise and significant information pertaining to communications technology. More than 30,000 communications users now receive *The Lenkurt Demodulator* – in over eighty countries throughout the world.

Write or call Lenkurt Electric Co., Inc., San Carlos, California. Or one of our Field Engineers in Washington, D.C., Lexington, Mass., Cocoa Beach, Florida, or Honolulu, Hawaii.

LENKURT ELECTRIC
GENERAL TELEPHONE & ELECTRONICS GTE

There was a time when Delta Star was the only business located north of Holly Street between Old County and Industrial Roads. The employee-owned company builds transformers, substations, and circuit switchers and breakers for the energy industry. The Spanish-style building in the foreground serves as the company's administrative offices. Today Delta Star is one of the largest employers in the city, with more than 170 on its payroll. (Delta Star.)

In 1946, William H. Kelly and William E. Moore started a business to supply professional painting contractors with the tools of their trade. The pair began with a store and warehouse at 789 Old County Road, which was visible from El Camino Real. Although the facade of the business has been altered, the building stands to this day. (Kelly Moore Paints.)

Supplying the home building industry on the peninsula was a good business for Kelly Moore Paints. From the company's single location in San Carlos, seen here in 1949, they now have more than 160 company-owned retail locations and manufacture more than 20 million gallons of paint each year. The company employs nearly 300 people in San Carlos. (Kelly Moore Paints.)

Located in the building that formerly housed the town's second post office at 734 El Camino Real, Biber Electric got its start in the 1930s (see page 28). In 1946, the three shops at 734 El Camino Real were combined, and the tower marquee was added. In 1959, the business' name was changed to the Lighthouse. Descendants of the Biber family operate the business to this day. (Author's collection.)

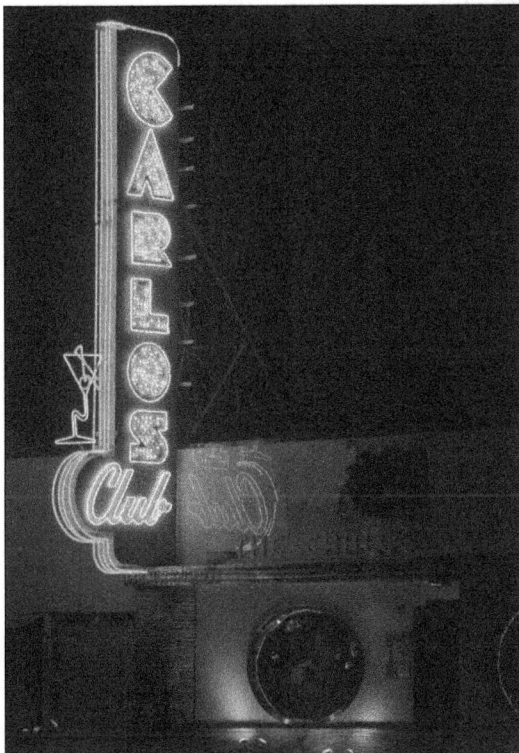

In the early 1920s, 612 El Camino Real was home to Tate's Restaurant and, over the years, was the site of a variety of bars. Owner Sydney Levin had the building refaced in 1947 as the Carlos Club. Prominent San Mateo architect Irving Caster's design was influenced by the art moderne style's use of a light green Carrara glass facade, glass blocks, speed lines, and large porthole-type windows. The Carlos Club remains a popular gathering place 50 years after its opening. (Author's collection.)

Carl and Louise DeBarbrie and brother Frank DeBarbrie and his wife, Theresa, built the San Carlos Bowl in the 800 block of El Camino Real in 1948 and 1949 at a cost of $155,000, which was a tremendous amount of money at the time. In 1955, the DeBarbries bought San Carlos Radio, at right, and the adjoining fish market to expand the bowling alley. (DeBarbrie/Gardner family.)

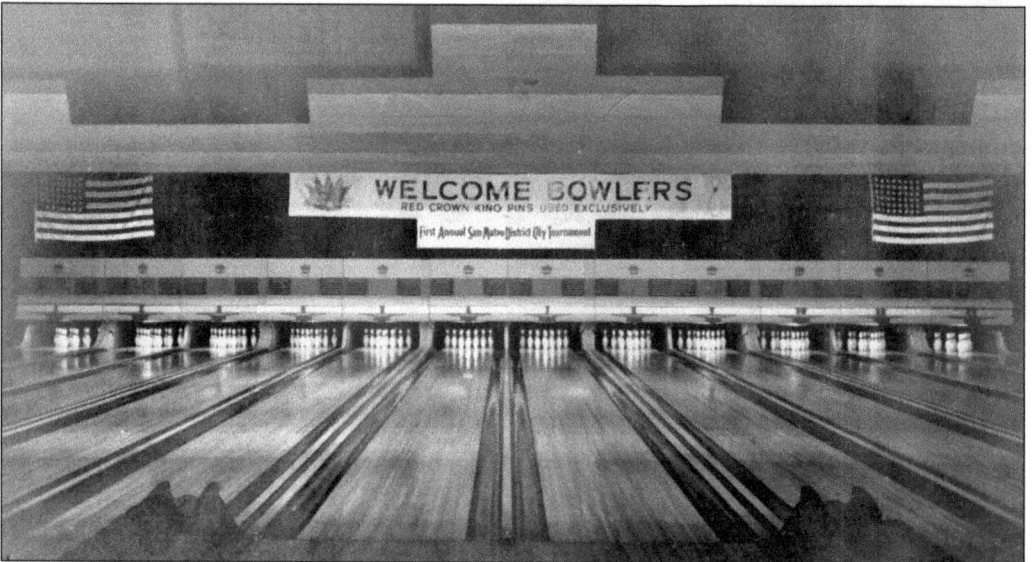

The San Carlos Bowl opened in January 1949 with 12 lanes and was a popular recreation spot for folks in town. The center also hosted numerous local and statewide tournaments. By 1955, adjacent properties were acquired, and four more lanes, a bar, and automatic pin setters were installed. In addition, it was the first Bay Area bowling center to have foul lights and automatic scorers. The San Carlos Bowl closed in May 1996. (DeBarbrie/Gardner family.)

The San Carlos Travel Lodge at 26 El Camino Real was built into the side of the hill on the corner of Spring Street. Note how the cars are parked facing Spring Street. This parking area has since been replaced with a nice swimming pool facility. The building with rectangular windows behind the Travel Lodge is 18 and 20 Laurel Street and remains to this day. The home next door with the pitched roof has been replaced by condominiums. (Author's collection.)

The San Carlos Travel Inn Motel at 950 El Camino Real was, at the time of this postcard (c. 1957), billed as the largest and finest motel in the city, with a heated pool and sun deck. Each of the 34 soundproof rooms had a radio and telephone, and rooms with televisions and kitchens were available. Oddly enough, while the Travel Inn's swimming pool has been replaced by parking stalls, the Travel Lodge's parking stalls have been replaced with a swimming pool. (Author's collection.)

Olsen Nolte Saddle Shop is a family-owned equestrian supply store specializing in English and Western riding styles. The store was opened in 1934 in San Francisco and moved to its current location at 1580 El Camino Real in 1959. (Author's collection.)

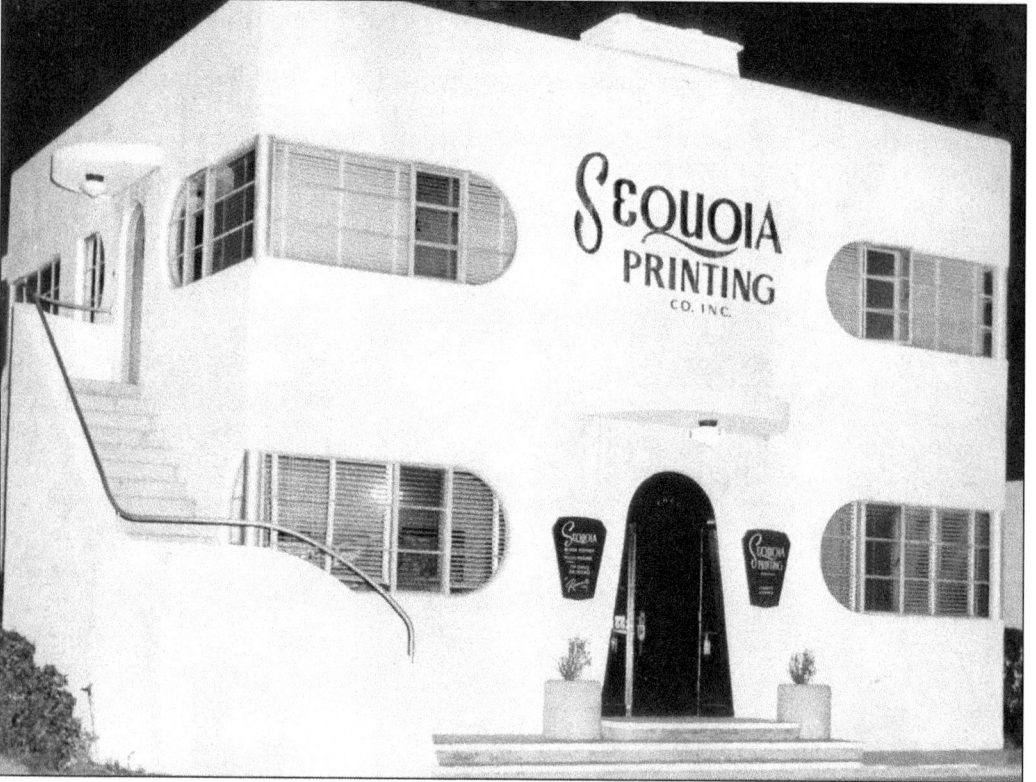

Originally built for Dr. George Hein in 1936, this streamline moderne–style building has seen a number of uses. Dr. Hein used it as both a residence and shop for his medical device business; the Varian brothers operated here; Dr. Pickels developed his ultra centrifuge on the property; it was home to the San Carlos Community Theater, the Peninsula Comic Opera, and the Little Carousel Theater; and it housed Sequoia Printing, as seen in this outstanding night photograph. Although the interior has been reconfigured for J&M Hobby House's retail operations, J&M's Cliff White reports that the building could easily be put back into its original state. (Cliff White collection.)

A Laurel Street location for Bank of America would allow the bank to expand and offer its customers greater parking behind the new building at 760 Laurel Street. In 1955, ground was broken for the new location by, from left to right, Edward Morley, assistant cashier; Budd O. Stevenson, contractor; Milton Lauterwasser, branch manager; Newell F. Sharkey, San Carlos City Council; Roland Risso, assistant manager; and David W. Mahaney, Republic Capital Company. (Newell Sharkey photograph via San Carlos Chamber of Commerce.)

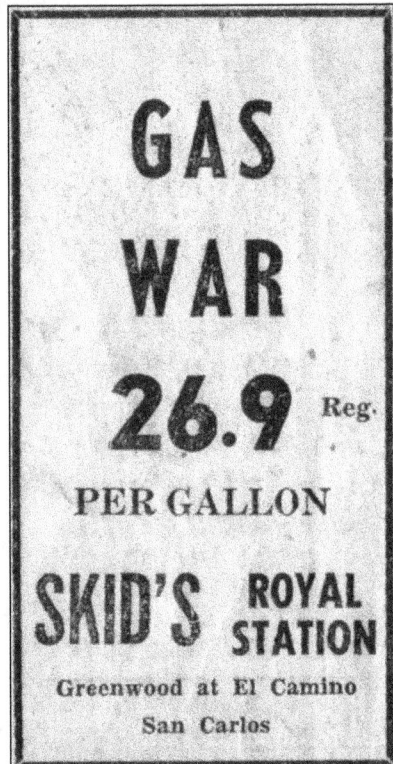

GAS WAR
26.9 Reg.
PER GALLON
SKID'S ROYAL STATION
Greenwood at El Camino
San Carlos

There was a time when gas was under 30¢ a gallon! That was October 16, 1957, when Skids Royal Station was competing with other service stations along El Camino Real for motorists' business. (Author's collection.)

The chamber of commerce was located at the depot during the 1960s. Gail Phillips is at the typewriter, and another young lady operates a mimeograph machine. The photograph was taken looking toward Old County Road. (Newell Sharkey via San Carlos Chamber of Commerce.)

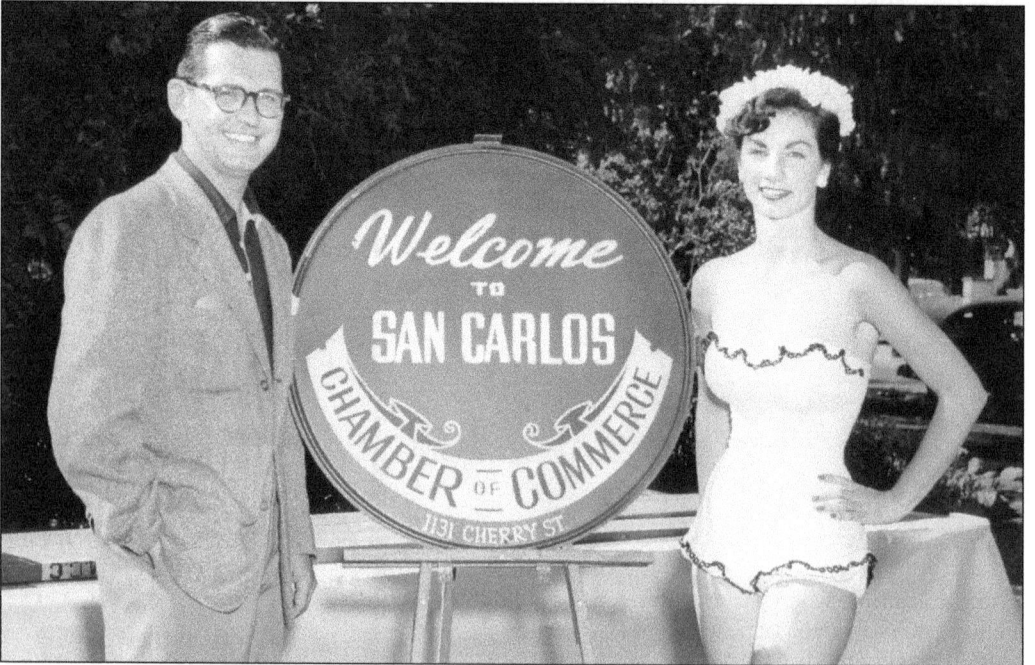

The chamber of commerce called 1133 Cherry Street home in the late 1950s. (San Carlos Chamber of Commerce.)

Donna Harding, Miss San Carlos 1963, promoted the "Program for Progress" to encourage membership in the Chamber of Commerce. (San Carlos Chamber of Commerce.)

Eureka Federal Savings was located at 1200 San Carlos Avenue. The company was one of the largest employers in San Carlos during the 1970s but was brought down after the industry was deregulated, with Eureka defaulting on more than $60 million in loans. (San Carlos Chamber of Commerce.)

73

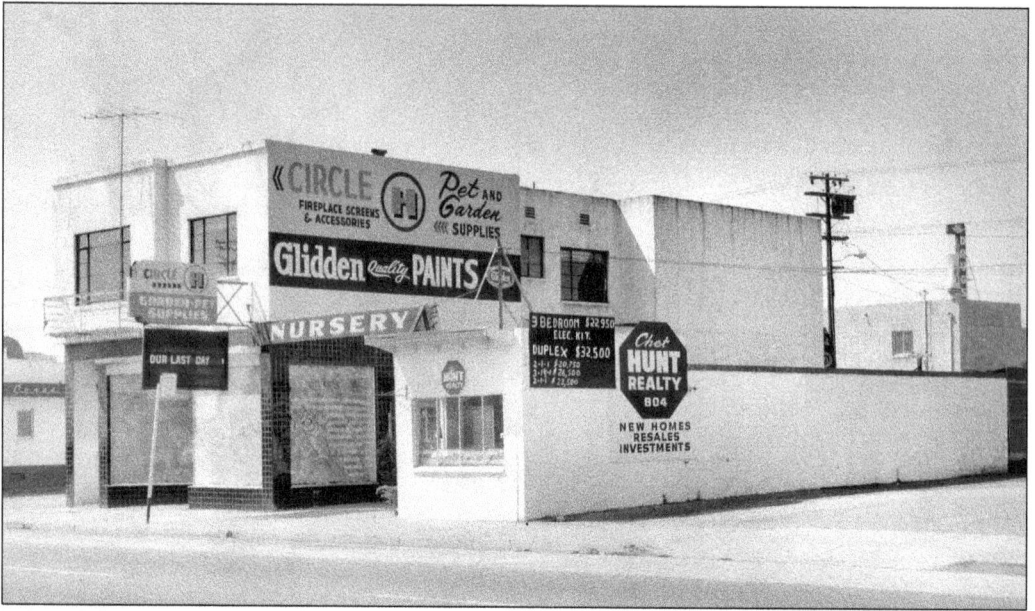

In July 1964, 804–806 El Camino Real was home to a pet and garden supply shop and a realtor. Chet Hunt Realty was offering a three-bedroom home with electric kitchen for $22,950, a duplex for $32,500, and two- and three-bedroom homes with 1 to 1.5 baths ranging from $20,750 to $26,500. After this photograph was taken, Fred Bausch acquired the property and converted it into the Clocksmith. Note the sign at right for the Arroyo Pharmacy on Laurel Street. (Newell Sharkey photograph via Bausch family.)

This rear view of 804–806 El Camino Real shows the parking area that was leased to the post office to store its vehicles. At one time, the building was home to Lee and Carole Pools, a pool sales company, and there was an in-ground pool located behind the trash-can enclosure. Note the Foster's Freeze restaurant to the right. (Newell Sharkey photograph via Bausch family.)

The Bausches' conversion of 804–806 El Camino Real resembles a cuckoo clock, with the upstairs becoming a residence while the ground floor has been transformed into a beautiful showroom for the sales and service of clocks of all kinds. The clock tower at the upper right corner of the building was added in 1984. (Author's collection.)

Baby Mart, a San Carlos landmark for more than 27 years, was located at the corner of El Camino Real and Howard Avenue. The grinning clown's face was painted at the entrance in 1953 and welcomed children, young and old, as they entered the store. The founder of Baby Mart, Abe Epstein, sold the store to Richard and JoAnn Mazzoni in 1970 but continued to own the building. As San Carlos prospered, rent for the building increased. With the introduction of Toys-R-Us and K-Mart to the area, the small, family-owned business could not compete, and the Mazzonis decided to call it quits, closing the doors in July 1980. (Rich Mazzoni.)

This image shows a typical mid-1960s view of the 1100 block of San Carlos Avenue. San Carlos became a stop on the Greyhound bus route in 1963, when Don and Marion Chase opened the station at 614 El Camino Real in the Carlos Club building. Next to Moe TV, on the north side of San Carlos Avenue, is Denny Williams Realty Company, which moved to this location in 1961. Williams, a San Carlos police officer from 1950 to 1955, still sells real estate today. (San Carlos Chamber of Commerce.)

The building at 1139 San Carlos Avenue is one of the oldest structures in San Carlos, predating the Drake Building. Shown in 1988, the structure was a local cocktail lounge known simply as the "1139 Club." The building now houses Vic's Family Restaurant in the lower level and professional offices above. (San Carlos Chamber of Commerce.)

Many beautiful brides from all over the peninsula made the drive to San Carlos to shop at Miss D's. Located at 1179 San Carlos Avenue, Miss D's reduced its square footage in the early 1990s and was gone by the turn of the century. The building now houses a Starbucks, Urbanization (a young women's boutique), and Plaza Florists. (San Carlos Chamber of Commerce.)

Schneider's, a family clothier, was formerly located on the corner of Laurel Street and Cherry Street, now home to a Blockbuster video rental store. Although a San Carlos institution for years, the dominance of regional retailers, such as Hillsdale Mall and the Target shopping complex in Redwood City, forced Schneider's and many other small retailers out of business. (San Carlos Chamber of Commerce.)

White Oaks Hardware has been an anchor store on the south end of Laurel Street since the 1940s. One of the few family-owned hardware stores remaining on the peninsula, White Oaks Hardware, at 1696 Laurel Street, provides a level of service not found at the big-box retailers. (Author's collection.)

The property at 825 Laurel Street has always been a pharmacy. The building was the Arroyo Pharmacy for years and has a great neon sign that can be seen at the rear of the building (see photograph page 74). In addition to prescriptions and other goods, today Siskin's San Carlos Pharmacy provides durable medical equipment such as wheelchairs. (San Carlos Chamber of Commerce.)

The City of San Carlos welcomes businesses of all sizes. White Oak Press opened its doors with a ribbon-cutting ceremony and fanfare to rival the large companies and city building openings. From left to right, Pete Nanarone, White Oaks Press owners Carrie and John Follett, Don Eaton, and two other chamber of commerce members cut the ribbon for the El Camino Real shop in 1982. White Oaks Press has since outgrown its first location and moved to 812 American Street. It continues to thrive in San Carlos. (San Carlos Chamber of Commerce.)

Inhale Therapeutic Systems, Inc., was founded in 1990 and changed its name to Nektar Therapeutics in 2003. Nektar is a biopharmaceutical company that develops drugs that are "easier to take, safer to use, longer lasting, and more effective." Nektar's corporate headquarters are located at 150 Industrial Road, and they have offices throughout the United States, as well as Ireland and India. Nektar is one of the largest employers in San Carlos, with more than 700 on the payroll. (San Carlos Chamber of Commerce.)

Architect S. Charles Lee's vision for the Carlos Theater was visually appealing, with its tall tower and framed marquee. The art deco exterior featured a number of portholes as well as unique vertical lighting to accent the building's facade. Space for two retail shops is included in this concept, a detail carried over to the final design. (UCLA Library Department of Special Collections/S. Charles Lee papers.)

Four

ARTS AND
ENTERTAINMENT

San Carlos has been a very rich and active city with regard to the arts. The city has housed three theaters: the Carlos, the Laurel, and the Tivoli. The Carlos Theater, located at 1224 San Carlos Avenue, was constructed in 1940, with its doors opening on January 11, 1941. The 817-seat theater had Saturday matinees that featured "kiddie shows," especially popular with the children. The longest-running film in the theatre's history was *Goldfinger*, which ran for more than two months. The theater, while still drawing crowds, was closed on September 17, 1976, and subsequently demolished to make room for an office building.

The Laurel Theater at 1500 Laurel Street was a single-story, single-screen theater in the art moderne style that opened in 1949. The theater closed in 1982, was demolished in 1999, and replaced with a mixed-use structure that houses office space on the lower level along Laurel Street, including the San Carlos Chamber of Commerce and a 42-unit apartment complex.

San Carlos' third movie house was the Tivoli Theater, located at 716 Laurel Street. The theater closed, and in 1989, the building was remodeled in the first major redevelopment project along Laurel Street, which saw the property converted into a restaurant.

The most notable San Carlos entertainment event is unquestionably the Chicken's Ball. The show began in 1940 as a fund-raiser for the school's milk fund and has continued as a biennial event ever since. The San Carlos Children's Theater, a nonprofit group established in 1990, provides children with acting classes and stage productions; it has introduced the arts to more than 2,000 children who have discovered they can be creative.

San Carlos also produced its share of A-list performers, including comedian and actor Dana Carvey of *Saturday Night Live* fame, Hollywood producer and director Katherine Bigalow, and actor/comedian Greg Proops, a San Carlos High School graduate most notable for his appearances on *Whose Line Is It Anyway*.

The Circle Star Theater was a nationally known venue that was located on Industrial Way at the border of San Carlos and Redwood City. The "theater in the round" was a 3,000-seat venue with a rotating stage. For audience members, there was not a bad seat in the house. Superstars such as Frank Sinatra, Sammy Davis Jr., Jack Benny, Liberace, Kenny Rogers, and Dionne Warwick, just to name a few, performed for the crowds. Many Broadway plays, such as *My Fair Lady*, *Vive Les Girls*, and *The Unsinkable Molly Brown*, were performed in the intimate theater.

The Carlos Theater was a sight to see at night, all lit up. The theater is seen here late in the evening during the first week of June 1941, with the Priscilla Lane–Jeffery Lynn–Ronald Reagan feature *Million Dollar Baby* leading the bill. (UCLA Library Department of Special Collections/S. Charles Lee papers.)

The opulent art moderne interior of the Carlos Theater featured sweeping scrolls throughout. The theater could seat more than 800, who came to watch films on the silver screen. (UCLA Library Department of Special Collections/S. Charles Lee papers.)

Central School, the only school in San Carlos at the time, was in need of a way to raise money for the milk fund. A Central School president and member of the PTA Board, Howard J. Demeke, came up with the idea of the Chicken's Ball, like the 1900s-era San Francisco Barbary Coast saloon shows. The Chicken's Ball of San Carlos was first performed in 1940 and raised $325. The production has been a biennial fund-raiser for San Carlos schools ever since. A collection of many of the Chicken's Ball programs are pictured here. (Morrison collection.)

Chicken's Ball skits are performed by local clubs, PTA groups, and individuals, all staying within the 1890–1918 Barbary Coast tradition. From left to right, Pop Burton, his wife Dina, George Seely, and his wife Lucille perform a skit in the 1958 production of the Chicken's Ball. (Seely collection.)

All stage supplies, props, and clothing for the Chicken's Ball are donated, borrowed, or handmade. Pictured here is an early skit by the scout mothers of Troops 151, 153, and 154. Note how spartan the set dressing is compared to productions of later years. The lack of scenery in the early days made it a focus as the productions grew. (Seely collection.)

The local police and fire departments were also involved with the Chicken's Ball. Included in this photograph are George Seely (fifth from left) and Eddie Wheeler Jr. and Howard Leal (seventh and eighth from left), both from the fire department. (Seely collection.)

A rehearsal for one of the skits is underway. This is a unique photograph because secrecy has always been a huge tradition for the Chicken's Ball, from the first show to today. No one, including reporters or other cast members, knows what skits are in the show prior to opening night. (Morrison collection.)

It takes a huge, coordinated, well-run volunteer effort to produce each Chicken's Ball. The 14 steering committee members pictured here manage an army of volunteers to produce a great show. Members of the 1998 Chicken's Ball Steering Committee are, from top to bottom, Melinda Johnstone, Kathy Dal Broi, April Pardini, Madelyn McWhite-Lamson, Joice Fong, Lesley Hoelper, Chet Moore, Jack Fisher, Dulcie Morrison, Laura Tyler-Jenkins, Lynn Ewing, Barbara Stogner, Nancy Martin, and Lisa Thompson. (Morrison collection.)

A 1970 Chicken's Ball skit by Dulcie Morrison, Audi Justus, Jena Nelson, and Lee Morrison is seen here. The Chicken's Ball is the longest-running school fund-raising event in the United States and is probably the most financially successful as well. (Newell Sharkey photograph via Morrison collection.)

Before the Chicken's Ball, the San Carlos Community Theater was the only creative outlet for the city's musically and dramatically inclined. Tickets were sold through Pasquale "Pat" Gianuario's Ideal Barber Shop on San Carlos Avenue, and productions were held at 1660 Laurel Street, in today's J&M Hobby House building. (Gianuario family.)

THE CAROUSEL LITTLE THEATRE

1660 Laurel Street   San Carlos

Presents

"THE GOLDEN AGE"

A Musical Comedy

By Margaret Price and Grace Cooley

FRIDAY, JUNE 8, 1951

Curtain: 8:30 P. M.

ADMISSION: 80c (Plus Tax, 20c) TOTAL $1.00

Nº 144

The Carousel Little Theater opened in 1947 and was located at 1660 Laurel Street in what is now J&M Hobby House. The theater was a very intimate venue, holding 160 seats, and showcased productions written by owner and manager Margaret Price. The theater was also the headquarters for the Peninsula Comic Opera Company and the San Carlos Community Theater. (Cliff White collection.)

Hollywood producers Sammy Lewis and Danny Dare opened the Melodyland theater in Anaheim, California, near Disneyland, in 1962. Using the Melodyland's success as their model for an "urban theater," Lewis and Dare opened the Circle Star Theater at 1800 Industrial Road in 1964. Billed as the "Theater of Tomorrow," ground was broken on March 6, 1964, and the entertainment venue opened its doors on October 13, 1964, in a full Hollywood gala-style event. (Author's collection.)

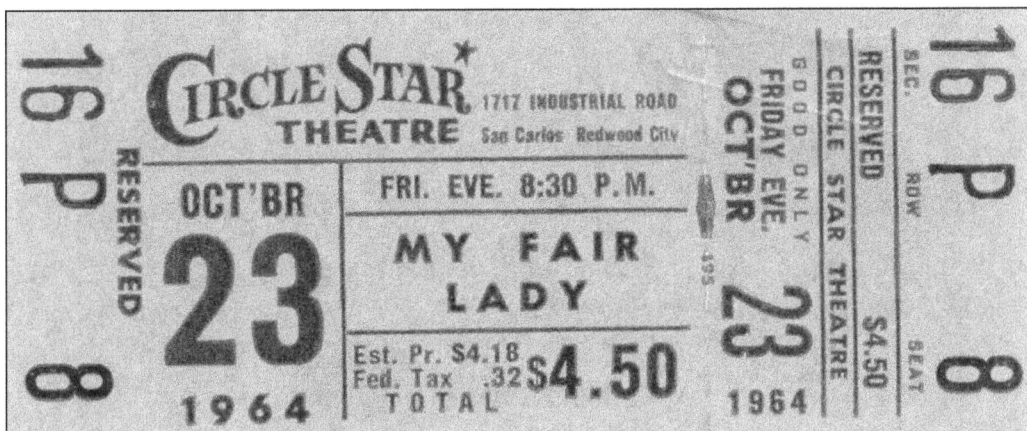

Pictured here is the program from the opening performance at the Circle Star of Lerner and Loewe's *My Fair Lady*, starring Jane Powell and Michael Evans. Section 16, Row P, Seat 8 cost $4.50. (Author's collection.)

Engagements at the Circle Star were limited to two weeks, but during the summer months, when audiences had greater entertainment and recreation choices, shows were often held to just 10 days. (Author's collection.)

90

Friday night boxing was big at the Circle Star. San Carlos's Ray Lunney III, pictured here doing battle at the Circle Star, won the National Amateur Athletic Union's 125-pound boxing title in 1970. (Reg McGovern.)

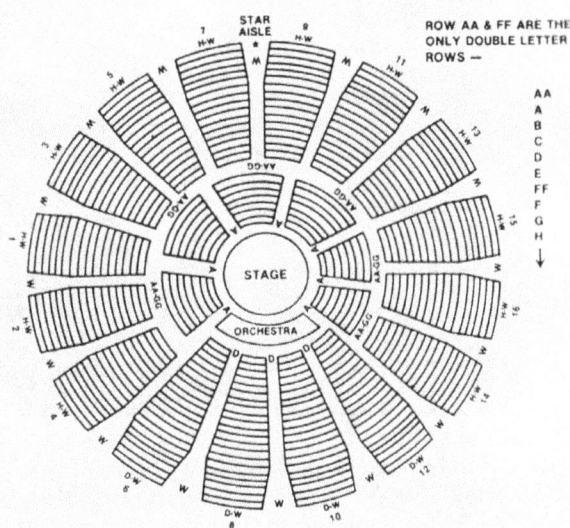

Circle Star Theatre

ROW AA & FF ARE THE ONLY DOUBLE LETTER ROWS —

The Circle Star was a theater in the round with a stage in the center and seating no further than 50 feet away from the stage. No seat was a bad seat, and the concept has been widely adopted over the years. The Star Aisle was the performer's entranceway to the stage. (Richard Vanderford family.)

Claire Everett Stewart was the daughter of Mr. and Mrs. E. E. Jones of Walnut Street in San Carlos. She became an accomplished ceramicist and clay artist, producing pottery under the Gaelic name "Sorcha Boru." Along with her husband, Ellsworth Stewart, they operated a studio in a 36-by-50-foot building on the corner of Holly Street and El Camino Real. She specialized in a variety of figures, such as this friar. (Vince Bravo collection.)

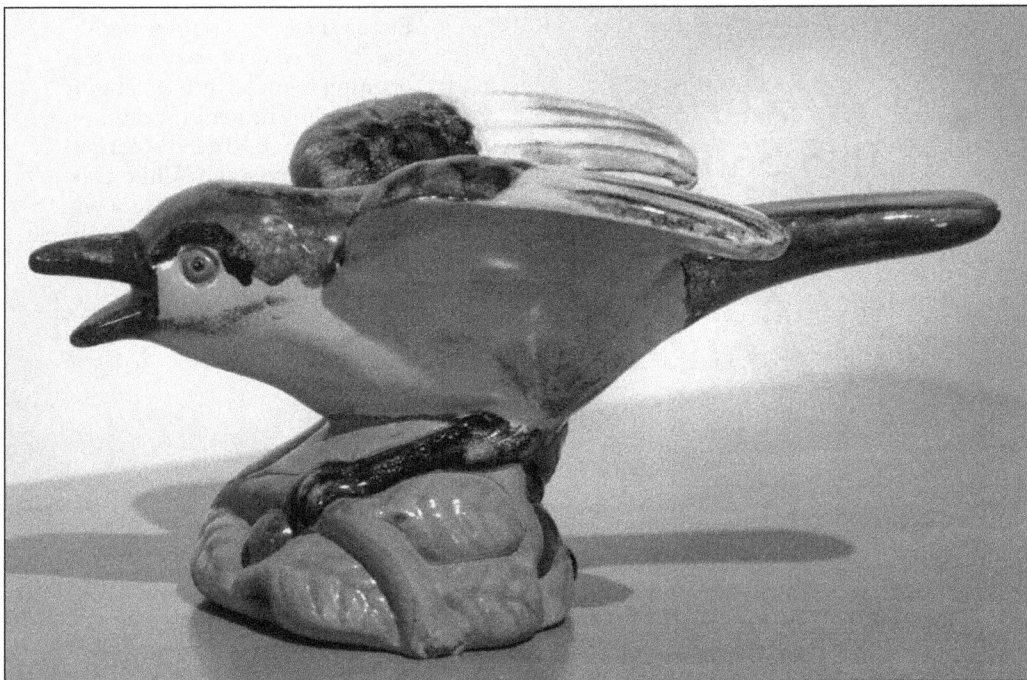

Sorcha Boru was widely recognized for her salt and pepper shakers as well as her depictions of small animals, such as this blue jay. (Vince Bravo collection.)

A most unusual piece from the Sorcha Boru studios is this San Francisco cable car with painted figures at the entrances. This piece is highly collectible and could be used as a butter dish or planter. (Vince Bravo collection.)

Pictured here is a reprint from the *Redwood City Tribune* of the opening night advertisement for the Laurel Theater on February 19, 1949. Located on the corner of Laurel Street and White Oak Way, the movie house was a big draw for businesses at the south end of Laurel Street. (Ken and Sandy Baisa collection.)

KTVU's Captain Satellite made a Saturday appearance at the Laurel Theater to entertain the kids. From left to right, the Captain is seen in the lobby with Karen Baeza, Ricky Coffey, Ricky Cramer, and Michael Cramer. (Ken and Sandy Baisa collection.)

In June 1980, the Laurel attempted a comeback. Family programming was the plan, but by 1982, the single-screen theater could no longer compete with multiplex cinemas and the new video rental craze. (Tim Davis Photography.)

After a contentious battle among residents, the developer, and the city, local residents won a small victory. Originally, the mixed-use development slated for the Laurel Theater property was to have a roof height of 50 feet. Neighbors were able to keep the building to four stories, and the project went ahead. (Ken Baisa.)

Kathryn Bigelow was born in San Carlos and graduated from Columbia's film school. She ventured to Hollywood, where she's written or directed some of best action films of recent memory. Bigelow penned *Blue Steel* (1990), *Undertow* (1996), and *The Hurt Locker*, which is slated for release in 2008. On the big screen she's directed *Mission Zero* starring Uma Thurman (2007), *K-19: The Widow Maker* with Liam Neeson and Harrison Ford (2002), *Strange Days* with Ralph Fiennes and Angela Bassett (1995) where she's seen on the set above, and *Point Break* starring Patrick Swayze, Keanu Reeves, and Gary Busey (1991), among others. On television, Bigelow directed three episodes of *Homicide: Life on the Street* and the miniseries *Wild Palms*. Other notable female stars from San Carlos include actress Rachelle Leah and actress/costume designer/producer Erica Engelhardt. (20th Century Fox.)

Emmy-award-winning comedian Dana Carvey, while born in Missoula, Montana, on June 2, 1955, moved to San Carlos with his family when he was three years old. Carvey attended Carlmont High School, then went on to receive his bachelor's degree in communication arts from San Francisco State University. While at San Francisco State, Carvey won the San Francisco Standup Comedy Competition. After graduation, he played several clubs in the Bay Area before moving to Los Angeles to pursue his career. Carvey went on to be a key member of *Saturday Night Live* for seven years, leaving in 1992 to perform in a host of entertainment endeavors, including the movies *Opportunity Knocks* (1990), *Wayne's World* (1992), *Wayne's World 2* (1993), and *The Road to Wellville* (1994). (Universal City Studios.)

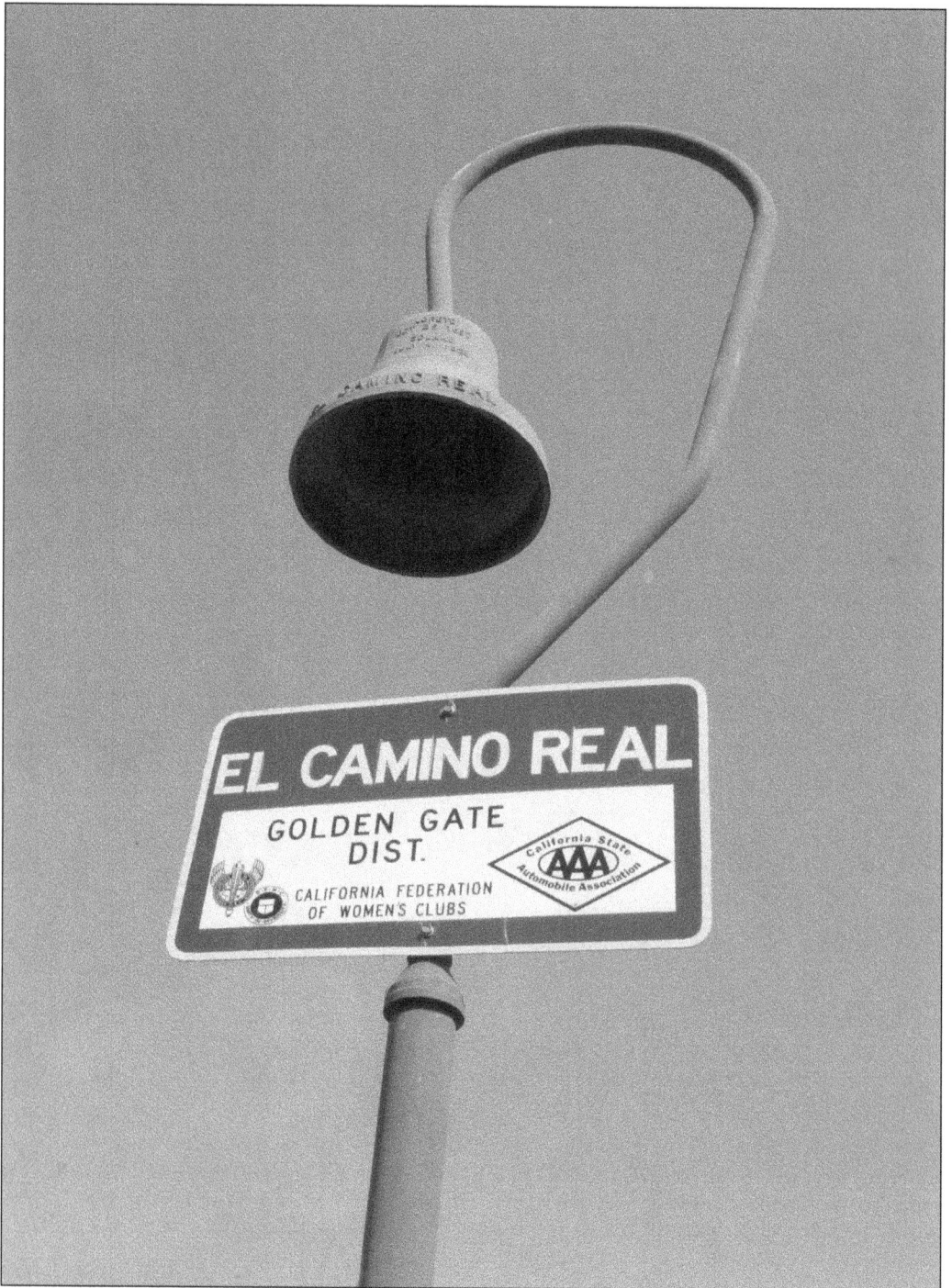

The California Federation of Women's Clubs began discussing the task of marking El Camino Real in 1902. In 1906, Mrs. A. S. C. Forbes presented a mission bell on a standard as a way to mark the route. Today two bells are located in San Carlos—one in the depot train station roundabout and the other on the El Camino side of the Drake Building on the corner of San Carlos Avenue and El Camino Real. (Author's collection.)

Five

PLANES, TRAINS, AUTOMOBILES . . . AND DOGS

San Carlos has had a long history with transportation, the military, and the racing community. Shortly before the town became a city, San Carlos was host to a one-and-one-quarter mile board track and later enjoyed a decade-long association with the Belmont Speedway, which was located on the city's border.

Beginning in World War II, a number of San Carlans served, and a number of local boys made the ultimate sacrifice. In addition, the city played host to a large number of servicemen housed at the War Dog Reception and Training Center, located at the top of Club Drive. On March 14, 1945, a navy R4D (DC-3) crashed at the top of today's Crestview Drive near Brittan Avenue. Seven died and 16 were injured in what was the worst air disaster in the city's history.

Less than three years after the end of World War II, the American Legion erected a building, becoming Post 585 and named in honor of Lloyd J. Tobey. One year after Post 585 opened, the North Koreans invaded South Korea and many San Carlans returned to active duty.

A decade later, by the mid-1960s, men and women from town were active in the Vietnam War. Vietnam veteran and award-winning author and playwright Tony Lazzarini is also from San Carlos. Lazzarini wrote *Highest Traditions: Memories of War*, which recalls his 21-month, 250-combat-mission tour in Vietnam as a helicopter door gunner with the U.S. Army's A Company, 25th Aviation Battalion. Eight men from San Carlos lost their lives halfway across the globe in Vietnam—Dana R. Kelley, U.S. Air Force; David W. Morrill, U.S. Marine Corps; his brother, Merwin L. Morrill, who served in the U.S. Air Force; Brock R. Schramm, U.S. Marine Corps; and Preston J. Snyder, John J. Tiscornia, Robert A. Van Patten, and Richard A. Vinal, who all served with the U.S. Army. Their sacrifices will never be forgotten.

San Carlos has had three airports during its history. The first was on property that bordered McCue Street and Old County Road. The second was alongside the Ohio Building at Steinberger's Slough, and the third is today's municipal airport on the east side of Highway 101.

San Carlos is also proud to have an astronaut call this city his hometown. Air Force colonel and NASA mission specialist Rex J. Walheim is a 1980 graduate of San Carlos High. He qualified as an astronaut in 1998 and flew aboard STS-110 *Atlantis* in April 2002. He is slated to fly again as a crewmember of STS-122, which will deliver the European Space Agency's Columbus Laboratory to the International Space Station.

The Greater San Francisco Speedway was a mile-and-one-quarter board track located on 140 acres between McCue Street on the north and Brittan Avenue on the south between Old County and Industrial Roads. The track had a 38-degree bank, and racers could reach death-defying speeds of more than 110 miles per hour. The first race was run on December 11, 1921, with a $25,000 purse. Here Jimmy Murphy leads Tommy Milton as Frank Elliott goes over the top of the track during the inaugural race. (Bruce Craig Collection/CH Motorcars.)

More than 40,000 spectators would come to San Carlos to watch the car races. The grandstands were located on the east side of Old County Road, where Arroyo Avenue is today. The stands were 1,800 feet long and 30 feet high. On June 18, 1922, fire destroyed much of the track. Only four auto races were run before the fire. (Redwood City Public Library.)

In October 1942, the U.S. Army came to San Carlos. A site, then known as the H and H Ranch (at the top of today's Club and Crestview Drives), was selected to become the U.S. Army War Dog Reception and Training Center. The first enlisted men for the army post were temporarily housed in the San Carlos Fire Station from December 15 to December 28, 1942. Each dog handler was given four dogs to train, and at the end of the course, the trainer selected the best one and shipped out. (Bill Carpentier photograph.)

Dogs were trained for the sentry, attack, scout, and messenger roles, and later to detect mines. In total, approximately 4,500 dogs were trained at the facility, and 1,200 could be accommodated at any one time. The facility was closed in October 1944. (Bill Carpentier photograph.)

LeRoy Gover was from a prominent San Carlos family (developers of the Gover Oaks tract). Young LeRoy had been bitten by the aviation bug, had begun flying, and acquired a Piper Cub in 1936. With war clouds on the horizon, Gover joined the Royal Air Force. He later flew with the American Eagle Squadron and is seen here with his P-47 Thunderbolt *Miss San Carlos* as a member of the 336th Fighter Squadron, Fourth Fighter Group. By war's end, Gover had flown 159 combat missions over Europe and was awarded the Silver Star for bravery along with three Distinguished Flying Crosses and eight Air Medals. Gover died in November 1997 at the age of 83. (Photograph from *Spitfires, Thunderbolts, and Warm Beer*, 1995, Potomac Books, Inc., formerly Brassey's, Inc.)

During World War II, women aviators and mechanics were trained at San Carlos Airport. Here, from left to right, Mary Keene, Billy Prior, unidentified, Enid Williams, unidentified, and Mary Terese Carey receive instruction from Bob Leavitt. (Redwood City Public Library.)

Pictured here is the ground-breaking for the American Legion Hall on Bush and Laurel Streets on February 2, 1948. From left to right are (first row, kneeling at right) Harry Peterson, Harry Humphrey, Lorenzo Jones, Bruce Allen, Harold Borchers, and Phil Glaves; (second row, standing) Harold DeArmond, George Lisher, Lloyd Tobey, Rita Borchers, Harley Watts, Richard Evans, Dugald McKeller, Howard Russel, three unidentified, Svend Nielsen, Harry Stanley, Howard Iams, unidentified, Edith Iams, Myrtle Grinnel, Roy Grinnel, Pierre Iphar, Lester Handcock, Steve Day, William E. Jones, and John Coss. (*San Carlos Enquirer* via American Legion Post 585.)

Dedication day for the post saw a parade through town via Cedar Avenue and a picnic at Burton Park. Today the post cares for a memorial garden and flagpole on the corner of Bush and Laurel Streets to honor those who have served the nation in time of war. (American Legion Post 585.)

On the property that is today PG&E, Ted L. Smith had built a racing oval. Four of Smith's friends joined the endeavor: Murray Baird, Al Florence, Perry Brown, and Frank Herman. Ground was broken for the Belmont Speedway on May 23, 1947, and three months later, on July 27, the first race was held. More than 3,300 paid to see midget racing on the track's first night of operation. (Ray Abrams collection.)

Stock cars were put through their paces at the Belmont Speedway on Wednesday nights. Note that the stands are nearly at capacity. (Ray Abrams collection.)

J. D. Mitchell gets another race started at the Belmont Speedway. To maintain safety standards, the Belmont Speedway motorcycle events were supervised by the Tri-City Motorcycle Club, which provided timers and other race officials. (Ray Abrams collection.)

Racing brothers Hugh (race 89) and Dick McAffee (race 88) were talented and popular riders on the circuit in the mid-1950s. (Pat Corner photograph via Ray Abrams collection.)

San Carlos did have a Harley-Davidson motorcycle dealership in the late 1950s. The Howard Overby Motor Company was located on Eaton Avenue and had its showroom on the ground floor. Maintenance was done upstairs, and bikes were taken up by elevator. Some chose, though, to ride up the ramp at the rear of the building. (Ray Abrams collection.)

In August 1964, the County of San Mateo was negotiating to acquire what is today the San Carlos Airport. The price was $990,000, which was a huge amount of money in 1964. Imagine flying lessons for $8.50 per hour. (San Mateo County Airports.)

Tail-wheel Cessnas and a Piper Tri-Pacer are seen in this late-1950s view of the San Carlos ramp. (San Mateo County Airports.)

In the mid-1950s, the runway was still not paved at San Carlos. When it rained, the field became a quagmire, trapping airplanes on the ramp for weeks. Today the San Carlos Airport is the mid-peninsula disaster relief site for airlifting supplies or personnel into the area should an earthquake close the freeways. General aviation played a large part in delivering supplies to areas cut off after the Loma Prieta Earthquake in 1989. (San Mateo County Airports.)

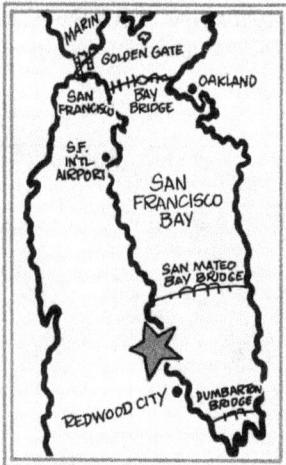

After the county had acquired San Carlos Airport, they began a marketing campaign to attract pilots. Cal-West Aviation, Inc., was the largest fixed-base operator on the field. Today the San Carlos and Half Moon Bay Airports generate approximately $800,000 in taxes that support the County General Fund, local cities, and school districts. (San Mateo County Airports.)

The San Carlos Airport is seen in this aerial view in January 1968. Note the large auto wrecker's yard at the south end of the airfield, and that Holly Street does not extend past the freeway cloverleaf. (San Mateo County Airports.)

After the Ohio Building was settled at the shores of San Carlos, the investors ran out of money. The building sat vacant during World War I; there were rumors of bootlegging and smuggling during Prohibition in an establishment called the Babylon Club. Another restaurateur tried his luck and failed, and the building was finally purchased by Charles P. Cooley to be used for workshops as well as research and development for his aviation businesses. After World War II, the structure sat vacant again. In order to remove the building quickly, on December 14, 1956, local fire departments set it on fire as part of a training program. (Reg McGovern.)

Radio personality Howard S. "Hap" Harper and a group of investors envisioned a restaurant, motel, and marina complex known as Harper's Ferry next to San Carlos Airport (see advertisement on page 108). Here the *Klamath* is being tugged to the airport site. (Reg McGovern.)

The man and his dream: Hap Harper and the *Klamath* are pictured here dockside at what was to become Harper's Ferry. Work has begun to add an entryway to the ferry. (Reg McGovern.)

By mid-1960, Harper's Ferry was taking shape. Harper's group of investors spent $35,000 to purchase the ferry *Klamath* and quickly poured another $170,000 into renovating the old ship. Harper's dream saw the ferry fitted with upper- and lower-deck dinning rooms, banquet rooms, kitchens to serve 850 guests, and a promenade area to stroll the length of the ship. Here the boat docks for the planned marina are in the works, and the *Klamath* is now landlocked. (San Mateo County Airports.)

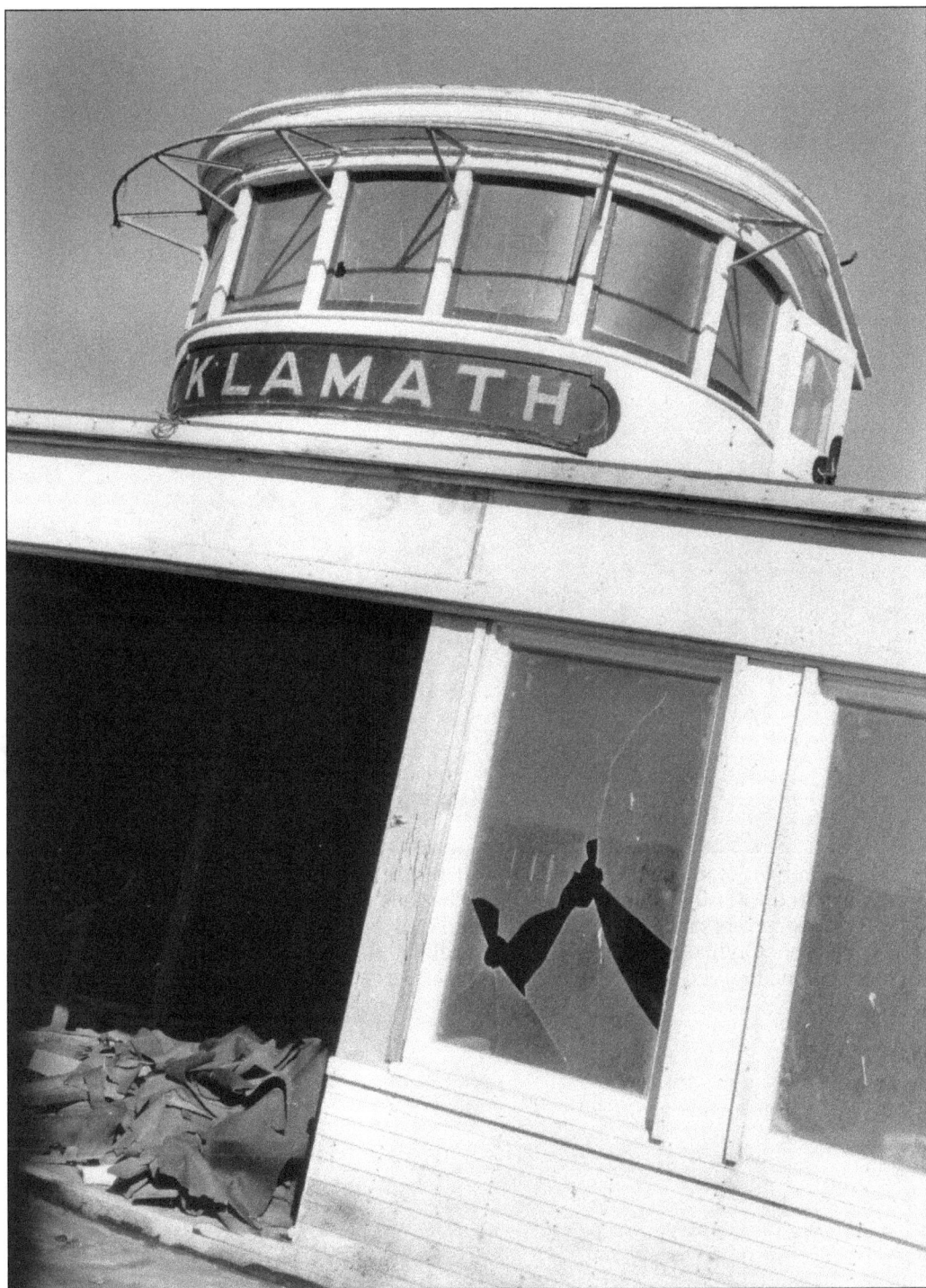

Harper's dream never materialized, and the *Klamath* became a derelict, the target for vandals. The old ferry was removed from its San Carlos home, and Hap Harper moved to the gold country to sell real estate. With that, the concept of having a marina in San Carlos was dead. (Reg McGovern.)

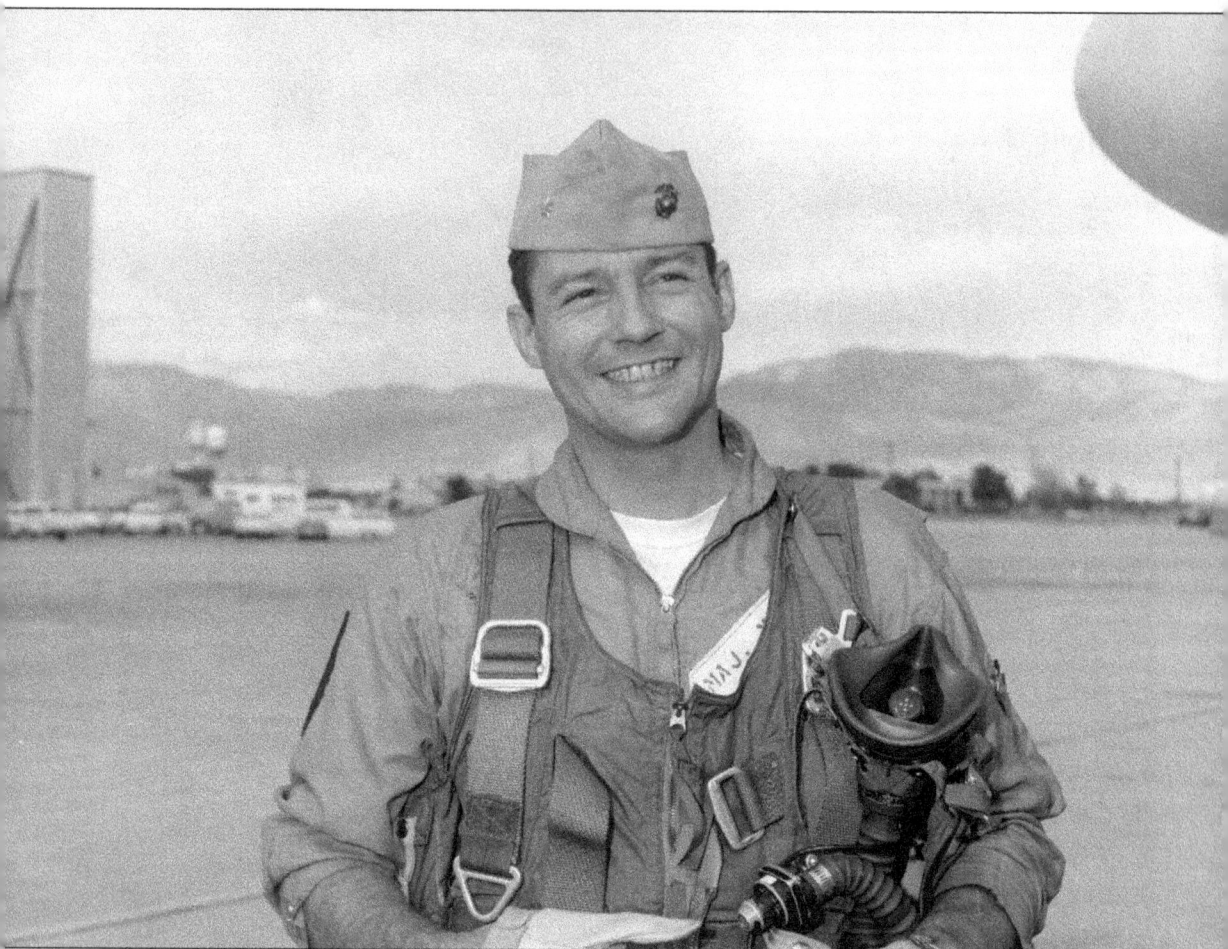

Brothers David W. Morrill and Merwin L. Morrill were both killed in Vietnam. David, seen here, was a major in the Marine Corps and flew F-4B Phantom IIs. On March 18, 1967, Major Morrill and his radar intercept officer, 2nd Lt. Charles Parker, were attacking an automatic weapons site near Kinh Mon. On his fourth pass, Major Morrill did not pull up, possibly because he'd been struck by ground fire. (David L. Morrill collection.)

U.S. Air Force captain Merwin L. "Mel" Morrill was flying an F-105D Thunderchief, Serial No. 59-1720, in a strike against the Yen Vinh rail yards near Hanoi on August 21, 1967. As he was leaving the target, Captain Morrill's jet was struck by antiaircraft fire, and he crashed seven miles south of the target. Captain Morrill was carried as missing in action until 1973, when it was determined he did not eject from his aircraft. On June 3, 1983, his remains were returned to the United States. (David L. Morrill collection.)

Richard "Dick" Vinal, who had played on the 1961 Babe Ruth World Series team, died in Vietnam on April 15, 1967. Vinal made it through a clearing, but his lieutenant was wounded by sniper fire and was trapped. When he went to help his lieutenant to safety, Vinal was killed in the attempt to rescue him. Vinal was awarded the Bronze Star for Valor for his actions. He left behind a wife, Susan. At home, the City of San Carlos dedicated the ball diamonds and scoreboard at Burton Park in Vinal's honor. (Marian Vinal collection.)

Space shuttle *Atlantis* (mission STS-110) delivered a truss segment to the International Space Station in April 2002. The crew are, from left to right (first row) Stephen N. Frick, pilot; Ellen Ochoa, flight engineer; and Michael J. Bloomfield, mission commander; (second row) astronauts Steven L. Smith, Rex J. Walheim (from San Carlos, California), Jerry L. Ross, and Lee M. E. Morin, all mission specialists. (NASA.)

Here is a nostalgic look from the early 1980s, when the train pulled up next to the depot as it had done for nearly a century. (Caltrain.)

By the mid-1980s, San Carlos residents were finding that the train caused tremendous traffic bottlenecks, extending the time it took to travel from El Camino to Highway 101. A solution was needed, and voters were willing to put their money where their complaints were and passed Measure A, which increased the county sales tax by one-half cent to elevate the trains. (Caltrain.)

The Belmont/San Carlos grade separation project stretched for 1.5 miles and saw the construction of new, elevated stations in both cities. The historic San Carlos Depot was not affected during the 42-month, $95.5 million project. (Caltrain.)

The grade separation project took four years to complete and saw the rail lines moved to the west side of the construction area. Trains operated on this "shoo-fly" while the track beds were elevated. The train is shown approaching Brittan Avenue at El Camino Real. The grade separation project was completed on June 8, 2000. (Caltrain.)

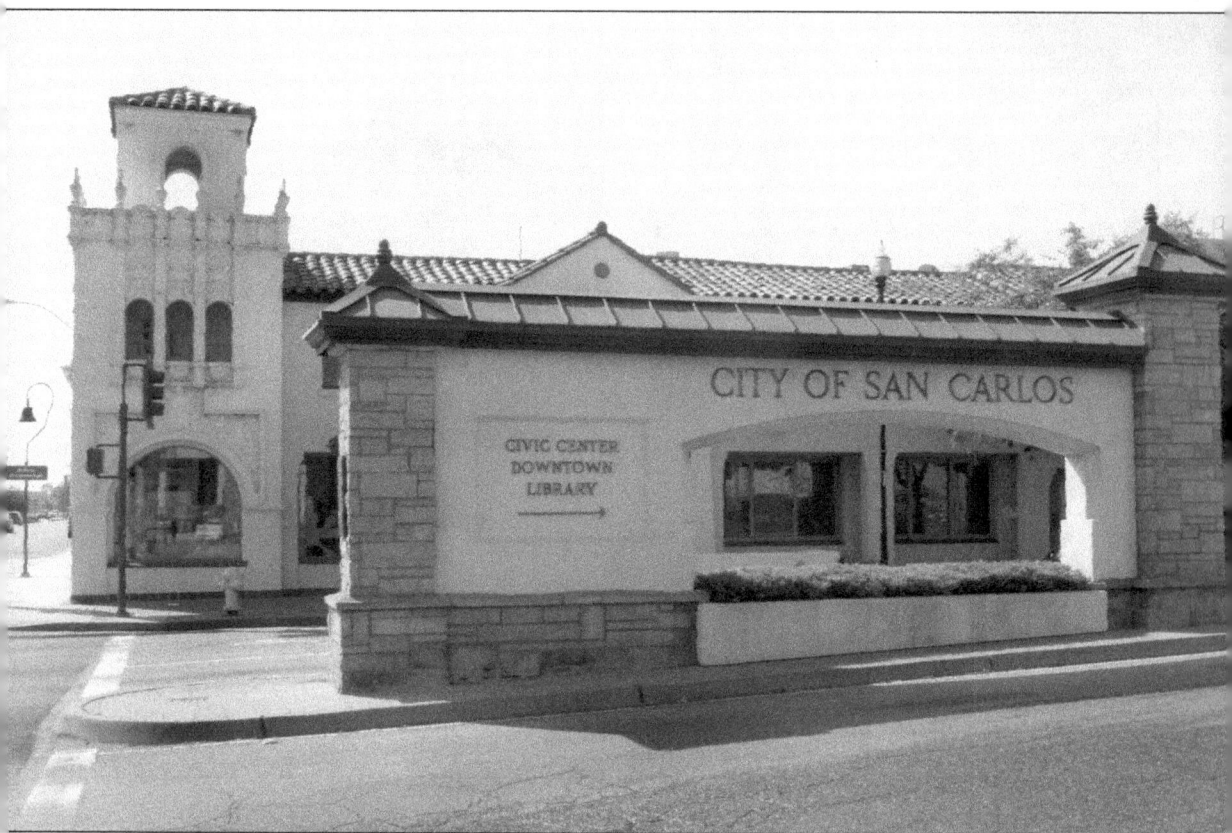

The San Carlos sign on El Camino Real and San Carlos Avenue, seen with the historic Drake Building in the background and an El Camino Real bell to the left, welcomes visitors to town and points the way to downtown, the Laurel Street shopping district, the civic center, and the library. (Author's collection.)

Six

SAN CARLOS TODAY

San Carlos has grown from the Spanish discovery of a small Native American village in 1769 to a city with a population of more than 28,000. The city covers 4.83 square miles and is located 25 miles from San Francisco and San Jose, in the middle of the San Francisco Peninsula. Fred Drake dubbed San Carlos "The City of Good Living," and that has not changed in all these years.

Today San Carlos is home to a nice downtown shopping district, many fine restaurants, excellent parks, award-winning schools, an airport and aviation museum, an adult center, and a youth center so the children have a quality place to gather, meet new friends, do homework, and play sports. San Carlos hosts many community activities, such as the Art and Wine Faire, Hot Harvest Nights, and Hometown Days. The city also hosts an annual garage sale, Art in the Park, and a summer concert series at Burton Park.

Over the years, San Carlos has been, and continues to be, home to industrial and commercial areas, technology firms, and biotech and medical instrumentation companies. Many light manufacturing companies have situated themselves along the Industrial and Old County Road corridors. These areas offer many industrial business parks that have a variety of square-foot-sized leases, which are perfect incubators for entrepreneurial endeavors.

Most of all, San Carlos is a great place to live. The climate is outstanding year-round, the people are friendly, and the city has been able to maintain its small-town atmosphere despite its growth.

The city held a ribbon cutting and dedication for the new San Carlos Library, located at 610 Elm Street as part of the civic center, on August 8, 1999. Cutting the ribbon are, from left to right, council member David Buckmaster, county supervisor Mary Griffin, Mayor Sylvia Nelson, council member Don Eaton, city manger Mike Garvey, and council member Mike King. The library can be accessed online through www.smcl.org. (San Carlos Chamber of Commerce.)

Located next to city hall in the Civic Center Plaza area, the state-of-the-art, 21,000-square-foot library houses an excellent collection of books, newspapers, magazines, CDs, books on tape, videos, business directories, consumer materials, and community information as well as public computers and wireless Internet access. The library also provides story hours, children's reading rooms, and special events throughout the year. (Author's collection.)

Many children who would eventually use the youth center were involved in the project during construction. Countless youngsters signed the building's beams as a form of time capsule for future generations to find. (San Carlos Youth Center.)

Completed and opened on September 7, 1999, the San Carlos Youth Center at Burton Park is a popular gathering place for preteen and young teens of the community (under youth development at www.cityofsancarlos.org). The facility includes activity rooms, a full-size gym, a television room, learning kitchen, dance studio, and homework center with computers. Money to build the youth center was raised by donations from the community. (Author's collection.)

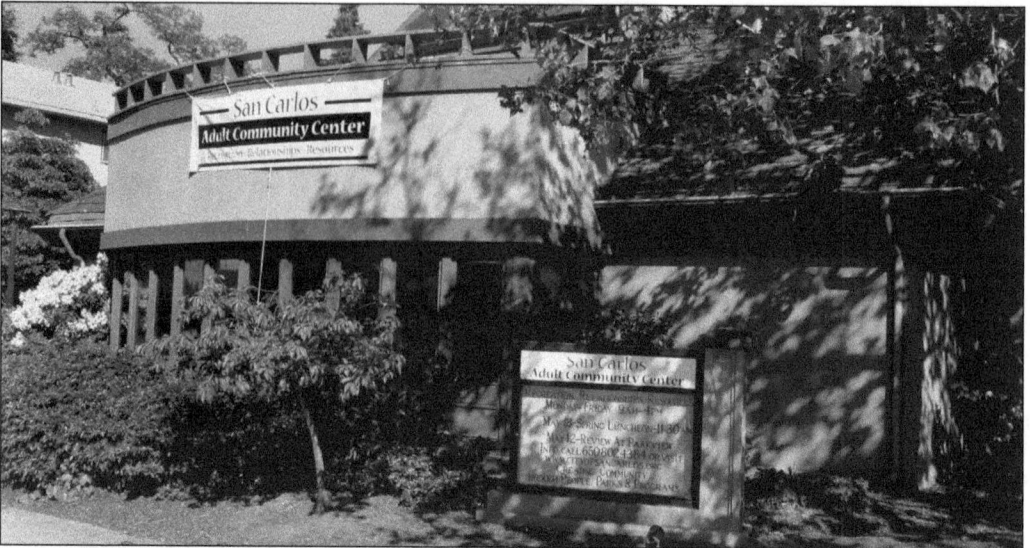

The 17,000-square-foot San Carlos Adult Community Center opened in August 1982, known then as the San Carlos Senior Center. The center provides recreation, classes, information, health screenings, and meals not only to San Carlos residents, but to all seniors 55 years or older. (Find them online at www.cityofsancarlos.org.) (Author's collection.)

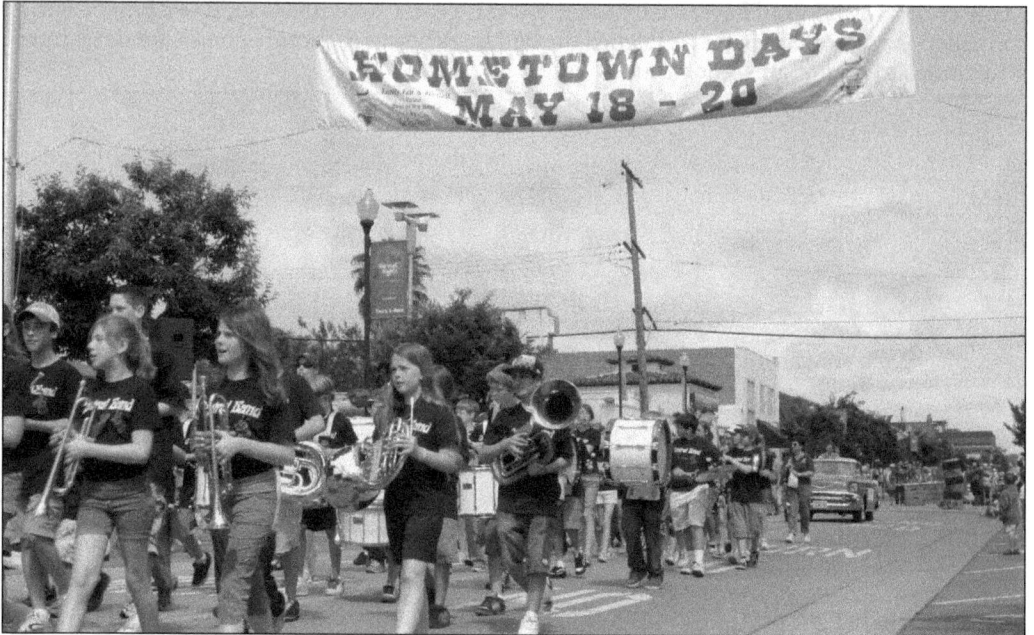

The dream of building community spirit and old-fashioned camaraderie by then-mayor Pat Bennie became a reality in September 1980. With the help of many community members and groups, the Western-themed Hometown Days held its first event on a rainy Saturday. Despite the morning rain, a sunny afternoon and Sunday helped to make a successful event for the clubs and organizations manning the booths as well as the hundreds of community members who attended. The tradition continues with a parade through town, arts and crafts, community exhibits, food and games at Burton Park, a Saturday evening Kiwanis Club barbeque, and a Sunday morning Rotary Club pancake breakfast. (Authors collection.)

Located on the east side of Highway 101, the Hiller Aviation Institute and Museum (www.hiller.org) displays and educates the public about science and aviation technologies. Each year, the museum hosts the Vertical Challenge Helicopter Air Show, which showcases how helicopters affect people's everyday life, from traffic reports to air ambulances and so much more. (R. Gozinya collection.)

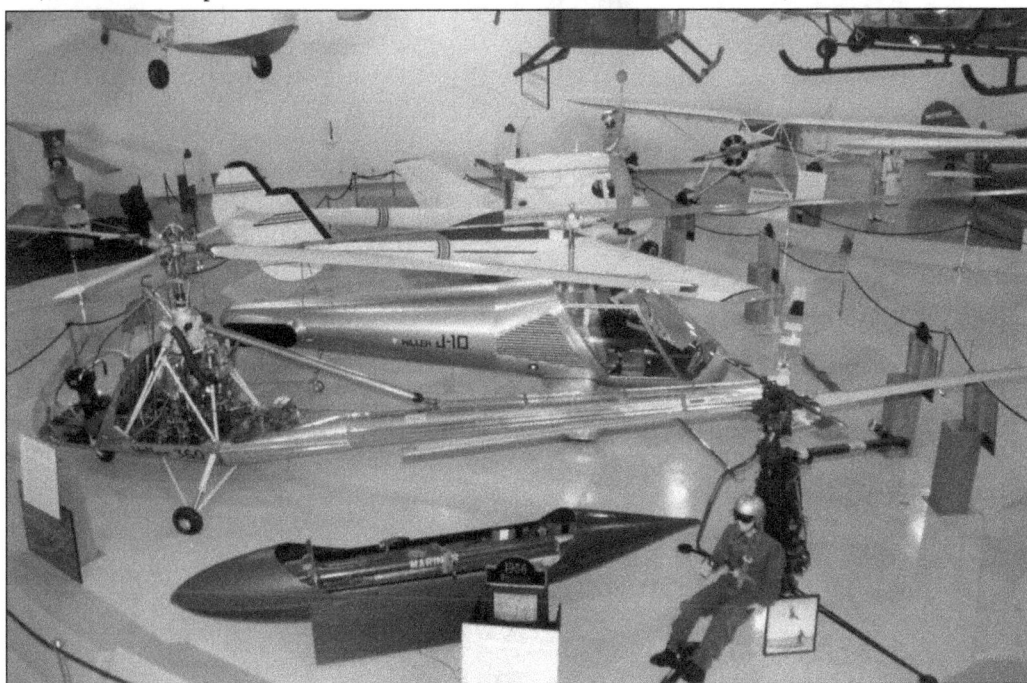

The Hiller Aviation Institute and Museum holds a phenomenal collection of aircraft and rotorcraft, many designed by museum namesake Stanley Hiller. Pictured here are a pusher-propeller Stearman-Hammond Y-1S (at the top of the photograph) built in Burlingame; a Hiller J-10, a no-tail-rotor design from the 1950s; a Hiller 360, which became the army UH-12; and, at the bottom, a Hiller Rotorcycle intended to be dropped to downed military pilots, who would assemble the craft and fly to safety. (Roger Cain.)

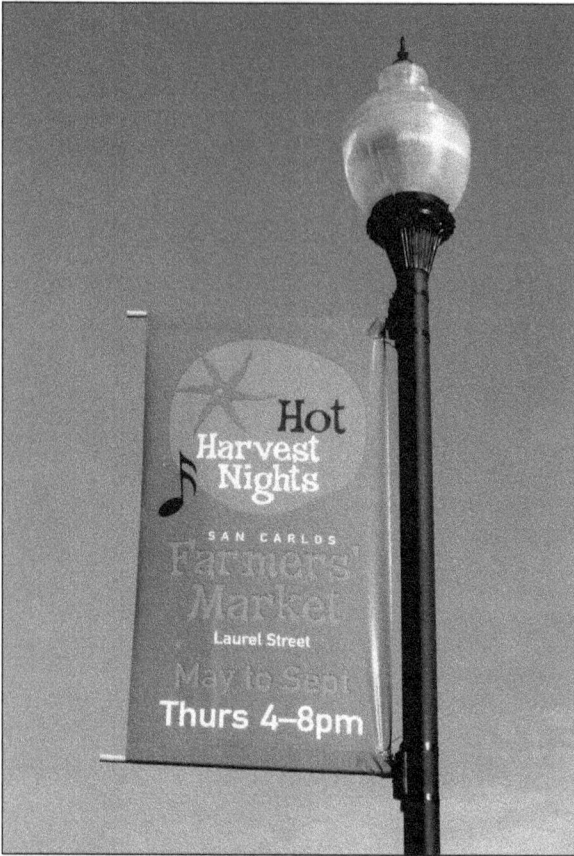

Presented by the San Carlos Chamber of Commerce, San Carlos Redevelopment Agency, and the Pacific Coast Farmers' Market Association, the 700 block of Laurel Street is transformed into a produce market and entertainment venue. Hot Harvest Nights, as it is known, is held every Thursday night from 4:00 to 8:00 p.m., May through September. Each week, along with the many produce and flower stands, the event spotlights four local businesses (one or two retail businesses, a service establishment or two, or a local nonprofit group). A different musical group plays in the Laurel Street Park each week, and the local shops stay open late. Pictured here is Jo Anne Montoya, a local resident, enjoying the selection of fresh produce. Hot Harvest Nights has evolved into a fun tradition for many local families. (R. Gozinya collection.)

Hosted by the San Carlos Chamber of Commerce (www.sancarloschamber.org), the Art and Wine Faire began in 1990. Held in October each year, the faire has grown to include an area from Laurel Street at Arroyo Avenue to San Carlos Avenue and from Walnut Street east to El Camino Real. (San Carlos Chamber of Commerce.)

The San Carlos Art and Wine Faire offers fairgoers a variety of high-quality items, including watercolor and oil paintings, photography, pottery, ceramics, wood working, and jewelry of many types. There are also a variety of wines and microbrews, food booths featuring international delights, a family fun zone, hands-on activities for the kids, and Italian street painters. (San Carlos Chamber of Commerce.)

Visit us at
arcadiapublishing.com